AIRCRA

BY F

Photo: Vandyk

THE AUTHOR

R. A. Saville-Sneath was born in Sheffield in 1895 and served in the
First World War as R. E. "Signals" motor-cyclist dispatch rider.

When he later became chairman of companies concerned with
aircraft equipment and international patent development, his pro-
fessional interests kept him in close touch with the trend of aircraft
design after the war. In July 1938 he was appointed Head Observer
at a local post of the Observer Corps, at that time a branch of the
Special Constabulary. Although familiar as an amateur pilot with
many types of aircraft, he found aircraft recognition to be a growing problem, requiring serious study and methodical instruction.

He gave many lectures on aircraft recognition and was an
honorary instructor and librarian for the Hearkers' Clubs. He
contributed articles on the subject to the *Daily Mail*, the *Daily
Mirror*, the *Aeroplane Spotter*, *Practical Mechanics* and other
journals. He was also the author of *British Aircraft* (2 vols.),
Aircraft of the United States (2 vols.) and *Britain's Airpower*.

R. A. Saville-Sneath was married and had three children. He
died in 1989.

A PENGUIN SPECIAL

AIRCRAFT RECOGNITION

BY
R. A. SAVILLE-SNEATH

PENGUIN BOOKS
HARMONDSWORTH MIDDLESEX ENGLAND

PENGUIN BOOKS

Published by the Penguin Group
27 Wrights Lane, London W8 5TZ, England
Viking Penguin Inc., 40 West 23rd Street, New York, New York 10010, USA
Penguin Books Australia Ltd, Ringwood, Victoria, Australia
Penguin Books Canada Ltd, 2801 John Street, Markham, Ontario, Canada L3R 1B4
Penguin Books (NZ) Ltd, 182–190 Wairau Road, Auckland 10, New Zealand

Penguin Books Ltd, Registered Offices: Harmondsworth, Middlesex, England

First published 1941
Facsimile Edition published 1990
1 3 5 7 9 10 8 6 4 2

Copyright 1941 by R. A. Saville-Sneath
Foreword to the Facsimile Edition © William Green, 1990
All rights reserved

Printed and bound in Great Britain by
Butler & Tanner Ltd, Frome and London

Foreword to the 1990 Facsimile Edition
by William Green

"One of theirs or one of ours ...?" How many times was that question to be uttered on the approach of an aircraft during the early forties? Its answer was, at times, truly a matter of life or death. Yet, when World War II commenced, the study of aircraft recognition had been largely neglected since the previous conflict, and what tuitional material *was* available was both sparse and unimaginative. As a consequence of this neglect, the opening stages of World War II witnessed innumerable instances of aircraft being fired upon by friendly ground forces, and even, at times, by friendly aircraft!

In fact, the importance of accurately identifying aircraft had been recognised during World War I, outline drawings of the most widely used aeroplanes of the opposing sides being issued to anti-aircraft gunners and others concerned. One of the first books to be devoted to aircraft recognition, *The Aircraft Identification Book* by R. Barlase Matthews and G. T. Clarkson, was published early in 1919, providing rudimentary outline drawings of the more common aircraft flying at that time. Between the wars, however, aircraft recognition did not, despite the immense crowds that flocked to air displays, capture the public imagination, and it was certainly not considered a specialised field of study by the authorities.

The Battle of Britain and the many tragic losses resulting from a general inability to differentiate between friend and foe underlined the importance of accurately identifying aircraft, and also exposed the inadequacies of aircraft recognition instruction. The services' handbook on the subject, *Air Publication 1480*, was of loose-leaf form and offered four-view silhouette drawings and, in some instances, poorly retouched flying photographs. But *A.P. 1480* was in short supply, and there was comparatively little else. Then, in September 1940, the first part of *Aircraft Identification: Friend or Foe* by E. Colston Shepherd was issued under the aegis of *The Aeroplane*, a weekly aviation publication. This slim booklet was, at two shillings (the equivalent of ten pence today), relatively expensive, but an attempt was now being made to cater for the growing awareness of the importance of accurate aircraft recognition.

Less than six months later, in February 1941, in the familiar Penguin orange paperback format, *Aircraft Recognition* by R. A.

Saville-Sneath made its début and proved an instant success, being both inexpensive and explicit. It was to reprint in April and May, successively revised editions appearing throughout the war years that followed. Indeed, it was to be printed in substantially larger numbers than any publication *to this day* devoted to the subject of identifying aeroplanes. Copies were soon to be found in the messes of every service airfield and anti-aircraft artillery site throughout the United Kingdom, on every Observer Corps reporting site and in the pocket of every Air Training Corps cadet.

Within its 174 pages, Saville-Sneath's *Aircraft Recognition* did not merely *illustrate* British and German military aircraft: it provided competent instruction in their recognition. It employed the contemporary four-view official silhouette drawings – the usual plan, head-on and side elevations being supplemented by a drawing at a flying angle – accompanied by copious notes on the special recognition points and principal features of the aircraft, grouped into categories. These groupings were preceded by sixteen pages of sepia photographs and half a dozen chapters intended to aid identification training, and were the end product of the author's long-standing interest in the subject, conceived while a motor-cyclist dispatch rider during World War I.

When Saville-Sneath joined the Observer Corps in 1938 it was the inadequacies of available tuitional material within this organisation that led him to compile *Aircraft Recognition*. He contributed regularly to the weekly (later fortnightly) publication produced specifically for those whose business or interest was the identification of aircraft, the *Aeroplane Spotter*. He also lectured on the subject, and this writer, who prior to entering the Royal Air Force taught aircraft recognition to the Air Training Corps, recalls with pleasure the enthusiasm and erudition with which he explained his tuitional methods.

Today, the identification of aircraft presents other problems than those of a half-century since, and the subject is much more sophisticated, including, for example, thermal imaging recognition – the recognition of the silhouette resulting from the heating of the airframe due to friction generated by the aircraft's passage through the air. Fifty years ago, however, the late R. A. Saville-Sneath was in no small part responsible for the evolution of effective methods of training in aircraft identification. Indeed, through the successive editions of *Aircraft Recognition*, he was possibly responsible for generating more interest in the subject than any other individual.

W. G.

CONTENTS

ACKNOWLEDGMENTS

The silhouettes reproduced in this book are Crown copyright and the author gratefully acknowledges the Air Ministry's permission to make use of them.

Similar acknowledgments are due to the publishers of *The Aeroplane, Flight* and *Jane's All The World's Aircraft* for kind permission to reproduce their copyright photographs.

The author also desires to acknowledge the courteous assistance of the leading firms in the aircraft industry in supplying photographs in such generous quantity that only a small proportion of them could be used on the present occasion.

INTRODUCTION

I

UNDER the special conditions of modern warfare interest in the identity of aircraft is not confined to members of H.M. Defence Services. A desire to be able to distinguish with *certainty* between friendly and hostile planes is widespread and natural. The continual growth in the number and variety of types in military use increases the complexity of the problem and suggests the need for a generally accessible introductory handbook to the subject. I have endeavoured to assemble the essential material in a form which I hope will prove both convenient and readable.

II

Many people, without conscious study, but possessing a trained or natural aptitude for observation, rapidly become familiar with the appearance of the types of aircraft most commonly seen in their own neighbourhood. Others find that the recognition of aeroplanes—even of types frequently seen—is unexpectedly difficult. Some will go so far as to say that aircraft, and in particular, those of modern high-speed monoplane type, resemble one another as closely as peas from the proverbial pod. This difficulty in recognising different types is very rarely associated with defective vision—in a literal sense. Generally, it arises from lack of knowing *where to look* for certain distinctive points which, to the initiated, are as obvious and as easily recognisable as the features of a familiar face .

This instantaneous, apparently instinctive, but *certain* recognition of aircraft in flight is the finished performance, the final stage of proficiency to which all training is directed.

7

The study of various types, "broken down" into their separate structural parts, re-assembled and mentally classified in the appropriate groups, is a necessary preparation for rapid progress to the desired standard.

III

It is customary to classify different types of aircraft according to any one of the following three methods :
   (1) Country of origin.
   (2) National markings.
   (3) Service function.
None of these methods is entirely satisfactory when considered solely from the point of view of aircraft recognition. These examples illustrate the inherent difficulties.

The American-built Douglas medium bomber, recently christened "Boston" by the R.A.F., is a militarised version of one of the latest Douglas air-liner types, D.C.5. A similar military version, designated A.20, is in service in the Army Air Corps of the U.S.A., and, as the Douglas D.B.7, the same type has been supplied to several other countries, including France. The fate of those supplied to France is uncertain, and it is conceivable that small numbers of them may have fallen into the hands of the Luftwaffe. Certainly other types of American-built aircraft, originally supplied to European countries at present under German domination, are known to have been used by the Luftwaffe in operations against Great Britain.

Standard types of aircraft built at the famous Fokker works in Holland have for many years been supplied to the Air Forces of other countries, including France and Sweden. After the German invasion of Holland, certain of these escaped and are now co-operating with the R.A.F. The Fokker works have probably ceased production as the result of the attentions of the R.A.F., but there is little doubt that a number of these standard types are still operating under neutral or hostile control.

The German-built Ju 86 air liner and its military version Ju 86K, two well-known types, are in service not only with the German Air Arm, but with the air forces of South Africa and Sweden.

8

Under these conditions, classification by national markings is as confusing as grouping by country of origin is inadequate.

If, in these dynamic days, we employ classification by function, a publication may be obsolete before the material has left the printing press. The biplane *fighter* of yesterday is a *trainer* to-day. The *day bomber* may become a *trainer* or may be transferred to *reconnaissance*; the *medium bomber* goes into service as a *twin-engine fighter* and the *heavy bomber* as a *troop transport*. Function depends upon new developments in design and upon the continually changing requirements of warfare.

Experience suggests that a system of grouping based upon the principal structural characteristics of an aircraft is most likely to meet the requirements of the service or civilian spotter, and this method is used in the present book.

It has the important advantage of bringing *similar types* together for easy reference and comparison. Thus, the Ju 88, which by reason of the similarity of its principal structural features is frequently confused with the " Blenheim," is precisely by reason of this structural similarity, automatically grouped with the Mk 1 and Mk IV versions of the Bristol " Blenheim."

For the same reason those " near twins " the R.A.F. " Bombay " and " Harrow " are grouped together. The American-built Consolidated twin-engine monoplane flying boat will be found in close company with its structural affinities, the British-built Saro " Lerwick " and the German " Dornier " flying boats.

The index provides, in addition to the usual alphabetical cross-reference, a brief description of the principal structural features of each aeroplane, in the form of a single line of readily understood abbreviations placed in a definite order.

By reference to the index alone, the country of origin and the principal structural features of each type can be ascertained. For example, against " Anson " we find :

I   GB   LW, E2, T1, Re, Ur.   pp. 60-1.

These abbreviations are expanded without difficulty to read : " *Structural Group I. Country of origin*, Great Britain. Low-wing monoplane, twin-engine, simple tail unit, radial engines, undercarriage retracts. Fully described on pages 60-61."

Much of the material assembled in the present book has been selected from a series of talks addressed to members of " Hearkers "* Clubs.

As these clubs are chiefly concerned with the study of air-craft recognition, a brief account of their origin and development may not be out of place.

Official arrangements for instruction in aircraft recognition, whilst excellent in quality, leave much to be desired in respect of quantity and availability. This circumstance, favourable to the growth of unofficial study circles, led to the formation in December, 1939, of the first " Hearkers " Club.

Founded by members of the R.A.F. Observer Corps in and around Guildford, Surrey, its objects were described as " the study and practice of all matters calculated to increase the efficiency of Observers."

The Hearkers' committee formulated standards of proficiency in aircraft recognition. They also created an appropriate certificate for award to members who pass their graded tests.

The founders of the club desired to see an increase in the instructional facilities available to spotters in all defence services, and from the earliest stages they have sought to achieve that end by enlisting the co-operation of the authorities.

Affiliated clubs have been formed in Croydon, Hendon, Liverpool, Evesham, Crowthorne and Southend, and many others are in course of formation.

I understand that the work of these Clubs may in the near future be officially recognised and assisted by a small grant, and that a proposal to change the name to " *The Observer Corps Club* " is under consideration.

January 1941.

* NOTE.—I am indebted to the founder for this account of the origin of the name " Hearker " : " In reply to an inquiry at the local inn for an observer, we were told that ' *'e be owt a 'arkin'*,' from which, I hope, the noun *Hearker* may be derived." (O. E. Dict. : " Hearkener." Old and Med. English.)

CHAPTER I

A SIMPLE STRUCTURAL GROUPING

ANYONE who takes the trouble to glance through the list of many hundreds of different types of aircraft in use to-day will need little persuasion to join with us in adopting a recent slogan of American industry, " Simplificate."

As a first step we disregard, for the time being, many aeroplanes which may *possibly* fly over Great Britain and concentrate upon some fifty or sixty of the principal military types of the R.A.F. and the Luftwaffe.

Of these, by far the largest number consists of *Monoplanes*. These can conveniently be subdivided into three distinct structural groups based upon the position of the wings in relation to the fuselage.

These groups are :

(1) Low-wing Monoplanes.

Fig. 1

Low-wing Monoplane : SPITFIRE

(2) Mid-wing Monoplanes.

Fig. 2

Mid-wing Monoplane : BUFFALO

(3) High-wing Monoplanes.

Fig. 3

High-wing Monoplane : LYSANDER

Continuing our grouping according to structural features, the remainder of our selection can be considered under two heads :

(4) Float Seaplanes and Flying-boats.

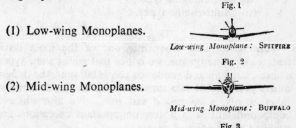

Fig. 4   Fig. 4A

Float Seaplane : HEINKEL 115   *Flying Boats :* LERWICK

(5) Biplanes (other than those in Group (4)).

Fig. 5

Biplanes : GLADIATOR

We find little difficulty in recognising the broad structural differences which distinguish any one of these *five principal groups* from the others.

Within each of the principal groups there are relatively few aircraft to consider and these, in turn, have clearly apparent differences in design. The most obvious difference from our point of view is the number of engines with which they are fitted. We therefore sub-divide each of the original groups into two classes :

    (i) Single-engine types.
    (ii) Multi-engine types.

TELL-TALE TAILS

Turning to tails, frequently one of the most distinctive features of an aeroplane, we notice that whilst some types have a single large fin and rudder or *simple* tail unit, the designers of others prefer to fit two somewhat smaller fins and rudders, in other words, a *compound* tail unit. We also observe that compound tails with a few unimportant exceptions are only fitted to multi-engined planes.

This very important structural difference enables us further to sub-divide the multi-engine types—which are rather numerous—so that we now have the following three sections within each of the five principal groups :

    (i) Single-engine types ;
    (ii) Multi-engine types with *simple* tail unit ;
    (iii) Multi-engine types with *compound* tail unit.

Fig. 6   Fig. 7   Fig. 8

Single-engine Types : *Multi-engine Types with Simple* *Multi-engine Types with*
HURRICANES   *Tail Unit :* JUNKERS 88   *Compound*
                                      Tail Unit : DORNIER 215

As examination of the various structural components proceeds, any early impression which we may have formed concerning the similarity of monoplane designs is replaced by astonishment at their extreme diversity.

Once this bridge is crossed, facility in aircraft recognition does not depend upon any rare or peculiar individual aptitude, but is simply a matter of regular observation and opportunity for practice.

PHOTOGRAPHS OR SILHOUETTES ?

Actual observation of aircraft in flight naturally provides the ideal form of practice, but we may find that the experience gained in this manner is unfortunately—or fortunately !— limited to a relatively small number of already well-known types.

We should also remember that the true spotter derives his greatest satisfaction from the identification of a strange type when it first crosses his horizon. Even though it may prove to be friendly, his feelings, if he fails to identify it on that critical first occasion, can best be understood and expressed by the golfer who fluffs his drive from the first tee.

We must therefore rely upon the use of photographs and silhouettes (and films whenever these are available) as the preliminary, if not the principal, means of acquiring familiarity with a wide range of different types of aircraft.

A word of caution is necessary in regard to the choice of photographs for preliminary study. " Close-up " pictures of aircraft may be as misleading and " horrific " as any seen on the screen. Taken at short range by means of a wide-angle lens they can be excellent as artistic compositions, yet grossly distort the appearance of important recognition features such as dihedral angle, taper and sweepback.

Photographs which show aircraft with lowered undercarriage, i.e. on the ground or during take-off and landing, may possess considerable general interest, but they are unsuitable for preliminary study. On the other hand, photographs, taken from a reasonable distance, depicting aircraft in characteristic flying attitudes, provide the best possible link between the fully detailed picture and the simple silhouette. We cannot have too much variety in our collection of this type of picture. Variety and frequent change are points which must be stressed, for the tendency to remember a particular type of aircraft by reference to some incidental feature of *landscape* becomes irresistible if the same photographs are repeatedly used.

In the early days of the Hearkers Club, photographs and silhouettes were used without distinction for instructional purposes and tests. Carefully selected photographs are still used for preliminary study and general documentation, but the Hearkers' graded tests are based upon recognition of *silhouettes*. This is a logical development, for a silhouette represents as accurately as possible the appearance of an aircraft in flight under average conditions of observation.

CHAPTER II

WINGS

THEIR POSITION IN RELATION TO THE FUSELAGE

WE have already seen that according to the relative position of the wings and fuselage a *monoplane* is described as of Low-wing, Mid-wing or High-wing type.

The Hurricane and Spitfire fighters are outstanding examples of modern low-wing monoplanes. Hampden and Wellington bombers and the different versions of the Blenheim are good examples of mid-wing design. The Hudson, although included, for the sake of simplicity in the mid-wing group, is intermediate between low and mid-wing, and is better described as a low mid-wing type. " Flying wing " monoplanes, an unusual type in which the fuselage is merged into the centre section of the wing, may for convenience be included in the mid-wing group. There are too few of them to justify special grouping.

| Fig. | Fig. 10 | Fig. 11 |

Low Mid-wing Type !
HUDSON

Parasol High-wing !
HENSCHEL 126

" Shoulder " High-wing !
DORNIER 17

Variants of the *high-wing* type are (i) Parasol High-wing

14

aircraft, in which the main plane is mounted above and clear of the fuselage to which it is attached by struts, and (ii) *Shoulder-wing*, a type in which as the name implies the wing-roots join the fuselage at the " shoulder," i.e. lower than the normal high-wing but appreciably higher than the mid-wing position.

The Henschel 126 is an example of the parasol high-wing type, this arrangement of wings being commonly adopted for reconnaissance aircraft of relatively low speed. The shoulder-wing position may be observed in the American-built R.A.F. " Boston " and in the two Dornier bombers, Do 17 and Do 215.

THE PLAN VIEW

Tapered wings predominate amongst modern types. Notable exceptions are, of course, the Spitfire wings of distinctive elliptical plan and the untapered wings of the Albacore, a modern biplane torpedo-carrier of the Fleet Air Arm.

The various combinations of straight edge and taper, together with the shape of the wing-tips, produce the characteristic wing silhouettes which are our chief recognition aids in the plan or overhead view.

The principal variations of wing plan may be roughly classified in the following manner. The appropriate abbreviation, P/0, etc., can be used to supplement the brief description which will be found in the Index.

P/0   Little or no taper ;

P/1   Moderate taper, approximately uniform on leading and trailing edges ;

P/2   Full taper, approximately uniform on leading and trailing edges ;

Fig. 12   Fig. 13   Fig. 14

P/0. ALBACORE   P/1. ANSON   P/2. HUDSON

15

P/3	Leading edge taper only ;
P/4	Trailing edge taper only ;
P/5	Compound taper ;
P/6	Elliptical plan.

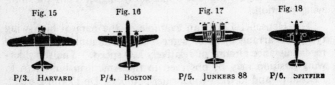

| Fig. 15 | Fig. 16 | Fig. 17 | Fig. 18 |
| P/3. HARVARD | P/4. BOSTON | P/5. JUNKERS 88 | P/6. SPITFIRE |

Sweepback is a characteristic of the wings which is clearly seen in the plan view. We should avoid a common tendency to confuse the term with *taper*. Sweepback describes the angle at which the wings are set—as viewed from above or below—rather than their form. Examples may be seen in the plan views of the Tiger Moth or the Stranraer, and it will be noticed that backswept wings may be completely without taper

Fig. 19

Sweepback is distinct from *Taper*
STRANRAER

Aspect Ratio.—The ratio of span to chord can only be regarded as a valuable aid to recognition when it is distinctly above or below the average, e.g. Wellington, Wellesley, Me 110 (high aspect ratio) and Whitley, Ju 89 and 90 (low aspect ratio).

Fig. 20   Fig. 21

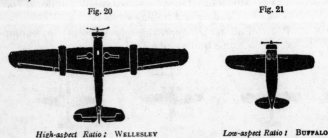

High-aspect Ratio : WELLESLEY   *Low-aspect Ratio :* BUFFALO

16

Span.—As the span of current service types ranges from 30 ft. to about 150 ft. we should endeavour to keep an approximate idea of this important dimension in mind. It is not only a useful recognition point which may be observed from many angles but it is chiefly upon our recollection of the span of a particular plane that the accuracy of our estimate of its height depends. In all cases where the information is available, the span, length and height are given in the descriptive section.

THE HEAD-ON OR STERN VIEW

Dihedral Angle.—The head-on or stern view of an aircraft is generally considered to be the most difficult to recognise. Fortunately, from an observer's point of view, the set of the wings of different aeroplanes varies considerably in relation to the horizontal. This angular setting, termed positive or negative dihedral angle, is naturally most evident in the full head-on and stern views.

The upward inclination towards the wing tips, or *positive* dihedral, is occasionally combined with a downwards inclination, or *negative* dihedral, near to the fuselage. The Junkers 87 dive-bomber shows this characteristic to a very marked degree, and in consequence is easily recognisable in head-on or stern views without other aids. The combination of positive and negative dihedral seen in the Ju 87 is known as "inverted gull-wing."

The ordinary "gull-wing," in which the arrangement of dihedral is the reverse of that just described, is less common, but the head-on silhouette of the Do 26 provides us with an excellent example.

Although the possible variations of dihedral are extremely numerous, we may usefully classify nine of the most usual forms. These are tabulated below, with typical examples selected from head-on silhouettes. The abbreviations D/0, etc., are suggested for use in conjunction with the brief descriptions previously mentioned.

17

D/0	Little or no dihedral;
D/1	Moderate dihedral;
D/2	Full dihedral;

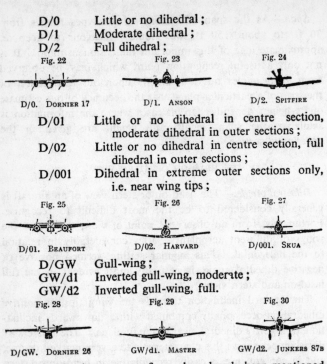

Fig. 22   Fig. 23   Fig. 24

D/0. DORNIER 17   D/1. ANSON   D/2. SPITFIRE

D/01	Little or no dihedral in centre section, moderate dihedral in outer sections;
D/02	Little or no dihedral in centre section, full dihedral in outer sections;
D/001	Dihedral in extreme outer sections only, i.e. near wing tips;

Fig. 25   Fig. 26   Fig. 27

D/01. BEAUFORT   D/02. HARVARD   D/001. SKUA

D/GW	Gull-wing;
GW/d1	Inverted gull-wing, moderate;
GW/d2	Inverted gull-wing, full.

Fig. 28   Fig. 29   Fig. 30

D/GW. DORNIER 26   GW/d1. MASTER   GW/d2. JUNKERS 87B

Span.—The importance of span has already been mentioned in considering the plan view. Its usefulness when the aircraft is seen from other angles is illustrated by the head-on silhouettes of Hurricane, Battle and He 113, which are here reproduced to the same scale.

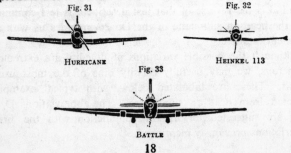

Fig. 31   Fig. 32

HURRICANE   HEINKEL 113

Fig. 33

BATTLE

18

CHAPTER III

ENGINES

As recognition aids, the number and the type of engines fitted to an aircraft rank almost equally in importance to the wings. Although the wings are usually the largest structural members and as such have a predominating influence on the characteristic appearance of an aeroplane, it frequently happens in practice that a plane can be definitely described as of single or multi-engine type, as the case may be, before the wing position can be clearly distinguished. This is particularly likely to occur when a distant side or plan view is presented to the observer.

Assuming that we have succeeded in distinguishing the *number* of engines, it should soon be possible to decide upon their type—whether IN-LINE or RADIAL engines. This feature is much more evident in single-engine planes since in their case the engine cowling or fairing determines the characteristic appearance of the nose of the fuselage. We see this clearly in the side views, the in-line engine giving the clean sharp nose outline, with low head resistance—a feature which is termed " clean entry "—whilst the larger diameter of the radial engine produces a nose of blunt or stubby rounded appearance. This aerodynamic disadvantage is offset to some extent by the fact that the radial engine is air-cooled and does not require the additional weight and complication of a liquid-cooling system.

Fig. 34   Fig. 35   Fig. 36

Liquid-cooled In-line Engine :
HURRICANE

Air-cooled Radial Engine :
HARVARD

JUNKERS 88 fitted with latest type of " Jumo " liquid-cooled *in-line* engines, the radiators of which resemble the cowling of *radial* engines

There is a notable exception to the general rule about the distinctive appearance of in-line and radial engines. If we refer to the silhouette of the Ju 88 we find that the engines, which are an unusually prominent feature, have the appearance of radial engines although they are in fact a new type of

Junkers Jumo liquid-cooled in-line engine which is fitted with a radiator of circular section.

The present trend of design in the U.S.A. may eventually reduce the sharp distinction between the two types. Twin-row radial engines, of smaller diameter than the single-row type, are in certain cases enclosed in cowlings which follow the clean, sharp lines which we are accustomed to associate only with in-line engines. As some of these types may sooner or later come into service in the R.A.F., we should make a mental note of them as further exceptions to our general rule.

Three-engine Aircraft.—These are uncommon (if we exclude those of the Italian Air Force), and this type should therefore present little difficulty. The Ju 52 is numerically the most important aircraft in this class.

Four-engine Aircraft.—Apart from two or three well-known types of air-liners and the Short four-engine flying boats, these are also comparatively uncommon. It is evident that careful observation of this point alone will greatly simplify our task since it will enable us to eliminate from consideration at least 90 per cent. of other types.

Twin-engine Aircraft.—In this very large group we may need every point which can be gleaned from observation not only of the type of engines fitted, but also of the manner in which they are installed. The engines are usually enclosed in nacelles, which may be mounted on the wing on their *centre lines*, i.e. with roughly equal parts of the nacelle above and below the wing. They may be mounted *above* the wing or more or less completely *underslung*. In comparatively rare cases, of which the Do 18 is a good example, two engines are mounted in tandem and from certain viewpoints they may easily be mistaken for a single engine.

We should also note the extent to which the nacelles project forward of the leading edge, their position relative to the nose of the aircraft and their setting with regard to the fuselage, i.e. whether parallel with it or at an angle. Finally, we should notice the after end of the nacelle, which usually terminates in a narrow streamline fairing. Should these fairings project *behind* the trailing edge of the wings, we note this as a relatively uncommon feature which will considerably facilitate recognition. (*See Fig.* 37.)

Many of these details may appear at first glance to have little or no importance. We should remember, however, that

Pointed fairings of engine nacelles
project *behind* the trailing edge of
wings : BOSTON

even when they cannot be clearly distinguished individually, they contribute to the characteristic appearance and " set " of an aeroplane which we shall eventually recognise without conscious analysis of its component parts.

CHAPTER IV

THE TAIL UNIT, FUSELAGE, UNDERCARRIAGE AND RADIATOR

TAIL UNIT

IN a large proportion of the aircraft with which we are concerned the tail unit is so individual and characteristic that it may almost be regarded as the designer's signature. Like the design of a car radiator which survives unchanged many modifications of body and chassis, the customary curves of fins, rudder and tailplane frequently persist through several of the aircraft constructor's successive models. This holds good to such a degree that many spotters experience no difficulty in recognising a number of current types from a view of the tail unit alone.

We have already referred to the broad distinction which enables us to sub-divide each of our five structural groups into the additional sections (ii) simple tail units and (iii) compound tail units.

The *simple* tail unit comprises a single fin, rudder, tailplane and elevator. The *compound* tail unit is usually fitted with two fins and rudders. Normally, these are mounted on the

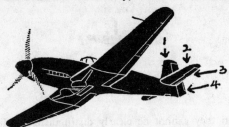

Simple Tail Unit: (1) Single fin, (2) tailplane (3) elevator (4) rudder

Fig. 38.—HEINKEL 113

single tailplane. Their position in relation to the tailplane varies with different designs. Frequently, as in many German types, they are placed at the extreme tips, and may be mounted with the greater part of their surface *above* the tailplane, as in the two Dornier bombers, or near to their centres, as seen in the Messerschmitt 110.

Compound Tail Unit: (1) Tailplane, (2) twin fins and rudders, (3) elevator, (4) rudder

Fig. 39.—MESSERSCHMITT 110

The Whitley bomber is an excellent example of the information which may be gained by a single glance at the position of the fins and rudders. These are placed roughly mid-way between the fuselage and the tailplane tips. They are braced to the fuselage—an unusual practice in modern designs. What is even more remarkable, they sit on top of the tailplane, with no part of their surface visible beneath. To a practised observer, they say " Whitley " in the clearest possible terms !

The well-known de Havilland four-engine air-liner, the biplane D.H.86 or " Dragon Express," a " simple tail " type, was modified by the addition of two small auxiliary fins, making three in all. As a result, D.H.86b, the modified version, has a compound tail unit of unusual and easily recognisable type.

Obsolete types of aircraft with compound tail units comprising *biplane* tailplanes between which two or three fins and rudders are mounted—the old box-kite arrangement—may still occasionally be seen.

The trend of current design appears to be moving away from the twin tails which have become a common feature of present-day aircraft, in favour of the simple tail unit. A recent instance is the latest Douglas forty-passenger, four-engine airliner, D.C.4. Built in small numbers and flown experimentally during 1939 with *triple* fins and rudders, D.C.4 has now gone into regular production with a single large fin and rudder.

THE FUSELAGE

We have already seen, in discussing wings, that the general appearance of an aircraft is very largely determined by the position of the fuselage in relation to the wings. Together they form the main structural framework.

When we first meet a new acquaintance the nose is often a feature which irresistibly claims our attention. So it frequently happens upon making our first acquaintance with a new type of aeroplane. We remember a nose which is round, another which is long and pointed and yet another which is square and squat. If at the same time we can retain a clear idea of the projection of the nose in regard to neighbouring features, we shall possess the first elements of a useful mental picture.

Occasionally the nearly vertical windows of a large control cabin show a distinct resemblance to the human brow, and the fertile imagination of an observer is not long in associating the facial outlines of different aircraft with those of his high, mid- and low-brow friends. It would be tactless to carry the parallel further, for " pimples " and " blisters " are terms commonly used to describe different forms of gun-turret. Certain German types of fuselage conveniently have a hog-like snout. (*See Figs.* 40-42)

The fuselage as a whole may be severe and rectangular in section ; of fine, slender streamline form, or short and round

23

as the barrel-like "Buffalo." In addition to these extreme types an almost infinite variety of intermediate shapes may be observed. The position and type of control cabin, cockpit,

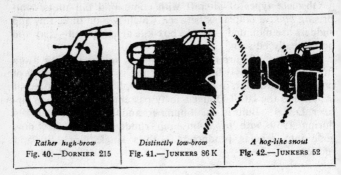

| *Rather high-brow*
Fig. 40.—DORNIER 215 | *Distinctly low-brow*
Fig. 41.—JUNKERS 86 K | *A hog-like snout*
Fig. 42.—JUNKERS 52 |

gun-turrets and any characteristic bulges which may be provided for additional armament or bomb-stowage are details which should not escape our attention.

In a few cases the shape of the fuselage provides the most obvious means of distinguishing between two aircraft which in other respects show many points of similarity. The Flamingo, for example, is similar in general arrangement to the Dornier 17. Both are high-wing monoplanes fitted with two radial engines and twin fins and rudders. The fins and rudders in both cases are set at the extreme tips of the tailplane and when viewed from certain angles appear to be of similar shape. But few of us could mistake the deep roomy fuselage of the British air-liner for the slender outlines of the "Flying Pencil" bomber.

THE UNDERCARRIAGE

During normal flight the undercarriage of a modern land-plane is conspicuous by its absence. It usually lies folded into the underside of the wings and fuselage, or in the case of multi-engine planes it may be drawn up into the engine nacelles. In the semi-retractable type of undercarriage, the lower part of the wheels remains exposed. This distinctive point may be clearly observed in some of the older types of service aircraft, such as the Anson and Battle.

When an undercarriage is observed to be heavily " trousered " or " spatted," i.e. fitted with streamline fairings which partially enclose the " legs " or wheels, respectively, we may reasonably assume that it is an undercarriage of the fixed type and accept this point as an aid to recognition. On the other hand, normally retractable undercarriages may be temporarily lowered during flight for a variety of reasons, amongst which we must include the possibility of ruse by a hostile pilot. The risk of mistaken identification will arise if, by attaching too much importance to the undercarriage, we permit our attention to be distracted from more reliable features.

It is interesting, for example—though not vitally important —to know that the Gladiator is fitted with a fixed under-carriage of cantilever type and that by this point alone it may readily be distinguished from the earlier Gloster Gauntlet, which has the older type of fixed braced undercarriage.

THE RADIATOR, ETC.

Under this head we may conveniently group those subsidiary points which are of interest in connection with general design, but which play no really important rôle in practical aircraft recognition.

They include such details as the position of the radiator of liquid-cooled engines, external gun-mountings, bomb-racks, dive-brakes, fixed or retractable tailwheels, tail skids, etc.

In some multi-engine types the deep radiators below the engine nacelles emphasise the distinction between in-line and radial engines. In certain single-engine planes the radiator is large and is so placed as to cause a characteristic bulge in the outline of the fuselage. To that extent observation of minor details may usefully supplement our view of more obvious features. If, however, a spotter were overheard to say that he recognised a Spitfire by the radiator installed under the starboard wing, it would be much the same as if he claimed to recognise his girl friend by the mole on her right shoulder !

CHAPTER V

AN ORDERLY PROCESS

WE have already seen that aircraft, far from looking alike, are subject to almost infinite variation in design.

Let us suppose that a wealthy sportsman, in time of peace, decides to commission a new monoplane, regardless of cost. He finds that he has a choice of three principal wing positions, low-wing, mid-wing and high-wing, as well as intermediate positions—say five in all.

Having settled this point, he may choose from one to four engines, or a larger number if he is prepared to depart from current designs. He will at the same time decide whether the engines are to be of radial or of in-line type. Thus any one of the five different wing positions could be provided with at least eight alternative forms of power plant, making forty variations in all. He may select any one of these forty variations with either single or twin-tail units, bringing the count up to eighty.

The fuselage presents endless possibilities, but we will suppose that our friend merely specifies any one of five distinct types : (i) slender streamline ; (ii) short and barrel-like ; (iii) large, with glazed " conservatory " ; (iv) single-seater with open cockpit ; (v) flying-boat hull.

Our initial eighty, multiplied by five, now amount to four hundred important variations in design !

Considering the wings, we have already classified seven distinct types of plan form, each of which may have at least nine typical variations in dihedral angle. Further, any of these variants may be set on to the fuselage with full, medium or no backsweep.

Let us check up our figures. We have noted $400 \times 7 \times 9 \times 3$, or 75,600 easily recognisable variations from which our friend must make a choice. He has also to decide between wings of high, medium and low aspect ratio ; between fixed, semi-retractable, fully retractable and float-type undercarriages. If the new craft should be a flying-boat it may have sponsons, fixed or retractable wing floats, or retractable wing-tip floats.

Doubtless by this time our amateur designer wishes that he had left these decisions to the constructors. Although the dimensions and colour are not yet determined, nor any of the minor details such as radiator and tailwheel, he has already made a selection from 75,600 × 3 × 4 recognition "points" or nearly a million major variations!

This little calculation demonstrates the need for an orderly mental process of elimination. If, on seeing an aircraft, we are able to say "low-wing type," we eliminate at one stroke four-fifths or about 800,000 "possibilities." When we note successively the number of engines and the type of tail unit, we reverse the process followed in building up our imaginary specification and speedily reduce the number of "possibles" to manageable proportions.

By concerning ourselves only with those types which are most commonly seen, we find, after this rapid preliminary "boiling down," only two or three alternatives left for consideration.

THE USE OF MNEMONICS

In view of the large part which memory plays in aircraft recognition it is not surprising that mnemonics—mechanical or indirect aids to memory—are freely used by spotters.

A good example of a simple mnemonic is that sometimes given to assist land-faring folk in using "port" and "starboard" in the right sense and to clear up a certain vagueness about the colour of the corresponding navigation lights: "*Red* and *port*, both short terms, correspond with *left*, which is short. *Green* and *starboard*, longer terms, correspond with the longer word *right*."

Or again, "to look upon the *port* when it is *red* is wrong (not *right*); therefore port and red are *left*."

Occasionally, however, mnemonics work both ways, for example: *Red* is a *left*-wing colour, but port has a distinctly *right* flavour.

To be really useful, they should be well chosen, ingenious and occasionally humorous. Mnemonics which we invent for ourselves are generally more valuable than those gleaned from others—they are more easily remembered!

In the early stages of training, many "Hearkers" use **WETFUR** set out in this manner, to assist them to remember the *order of importance* of the various aids to recognition.

(1) W ings
(2) E ngine
(3) T ail unit
(4) F uselage
(5) U ndercarriage
(6) R adiator, etc.

27

This does not imply that there is a hard and fast rule concerning the order in which these points should be noted. In actual practice that will necessarily depend on the attitude in which the aircraft is first seen. In a large proportion of cases, however, the order suggested by the mnemonic agrees with that in which the various structural parts are first observed.

Our imaginary specification showed that by the time we had fully covered the first five points we had considered nearly a million major variations in design. In general, observation of the first three points, remembered by the aid of the mnemonic W–E–T will suffice to confirm the identity of an aircraft, but enough exceptions are encountered to justify the use of the complete list.

The following simple mnemonics are quoted as examples of those currently employed. There are others, not so simple, which have a useful but essentially private circulation.

ALBA-CORE—Equal division of name suggests biplane of equal span. *Core* suggests centre-section cut away.

ANSON—'*anson* suggests a large cab with dickey seat over.

BOMBAY—B for *bean* suggests the typical bean or kidney shape of fins and rudders. B for *belly* suggests a prominent feature of the " Bombay " and its generally rounded lines.

BUFFALO (Brewster 339)—B for *barrel*-like fuselage. *Brewster* also suggests beer-barrel.

HARROW—H suggests straight lines, a feature of Harrow design, in contrast to the otherwise similar type " Bombay."

HENSCHEL 126 and LYSANDER—H for *high* tailplane of Henschel ; L for *low* tailplane of Lysander.

HURRICANE—H again suggests *straight lines* of " Hurricane " tapered wings and the absence of dihedral (*straight* wings). H for *humpbacked* fuselage ; -*cane* also suggests *straight lines*.

JUNKERS aircraft—*Junkers* suggests hard angular outlines.
Ju 88—*Ju* suggests jutting engines.
G 38—Gee ! Expression of surprise on sighting this four-engined " flying wing." 3–8 *three* fins, *four* engines and *four* wheels of undercarriage : G 3–8.

" LONDON " and " STRANRAER "—In order to distinguish
between two similar types of flying boat :

" *London*," shorter name, has considerably shorter span
than that of " *Stranraer*."

S of " Stranraer " suggests *s*weepback of " Stranraer "
wings.

" SPITFIRE "—S suggests (i) curved outline of letter S and
the " Spitfire " wings; (ii) *s*mall tail unit compared with
" Hurricane "; (iii) *s*tarboard position of radiator ; *-fire*
suggests resemblance to *flame* in elliptical " Spitfire "
wings.

CHAPTER VI

RECOGNITION BY SOUND

MANY hundreds of letters have been written to the lay and
technical Press on this subject. They indicate an almost
equal division of opinion between enthusiastic advocates of
recognition by sound and those who consider that aural recognition is either completely impossible or of no practical utility.
The correspondents quote many interesting examples in support
of their respective points of view. This division of opinion is
not surprising, for most of us can recall from personal experience different incidents which could be quoted to reinforce
arguments on *both* sides of the question.

There is much to support the view that recognition by sound
is not only possible, but that it may be developed to a considerable degree of usefulness. On the other hand, those observers
who by long practice have become most proficient in the art
are usually well aware of its limitations and are least prone to
make exaggerated claims on its behalf.

Many cases of supposed recognition by sound prove upon
analysis to be compounded of one part hearing and one part
inference. Certainly the distinction between comparatively
slow single-engine trainers and high-speed single-engine
fighters is very easily made by ear alone. But the conclusion
that such single-engine trainers are friendly is less frequently
based upon definite recognition of the individual " note " of a
particular British engine or aeroplane than upon the reason-

able assumption that hostile light training types would not knowingly venture to cross our coastline.

By a similar process of thought, the beat of a heavy twin-engine aircraft heard at night may with considerable conviction be described as hostile. It usually is so described and, in the majority of cases, correctly. So long as we are prepared to concede that the inferential part may now and again lead our judgment astray, and refrain from positive statement, very little harm will result from the occasional error.

The following incident illustrates the tendency—which long practice and proved ability in aural recognition does not entirely remove—to allow our impressions to be unduly influenced by the special conditions of the moment.

During a recent evening raid the familiar drone of enemy bombers formed an almost constant background of sound mingling with the crash of neighbouring guns and the intermittent crump of a stick of bombs. Two observers had just handed over to their relief crew, so that four men were present at the time. The telephonist, on taking over, enquired whether a twin-engine plane which could be heard approaching was, as he expected, hostile. Three experienced listeners unanimously agreed that it had " the heavy beat of a Jerry."

The telephonist at that moment received a report that a friendly fighter, a twin-engine Blenheim, was approaching, and almost simultaneously the supposedly hostile bomber gave British recognition signals. The men concerned had repeatedly proved their ability to recognise a Blenheim by ear alone, and there is little doubt that in this instance their assumptions based upon the prevailing conditions, allowing for the physical difficulty of distinguishing any individual " note " under those conditions, were stronger than any impression derived from a characteristic note.

Under more favourable conditions the ability displayed by some observers in identifying *British* planes by sound is really amazing. Albacores or Lysanders will be named—tentatively, it is true, because observers are wisely trained to avoid positive statement in reports based solely upon sound—when flying above clouds at heights up to 10,000 feet or so. The identification is verified either by subsequent reports or by actual sight of the aircraft as it crosses a clear opening between clouds.

The fine distinction between a Merlin-engined Hurricane and a Spitfire is considered difficult to detect, but the Battle, also fitted with a Merlin engine, is generally distinguished from either of these fighters with comparative ease. Ansons and Harvards are regarded as "easy meat." On one occasion, someone enquired whether "Limping Lizzie" had been seen in the district. The name was so apt that it was at once recognised as an allusion to a particular Anson.

The Wellington has a high-pitched note by which it is easily recognised at low altitudes. This note appears to be independent of exhaust noise and is probably aerodynamic. It cannot be heard by a ground observer when the Wellington is flying at any considerable height. Under these conditions the deeper notes, which carry further, predominate and the characteristic sound is completely changed.

The effects of height, cloud layers, reflected sound, cross currents, speed, direction and manœuvre upon an aircraft's customary note—which is a compound of engine, airscrew and aerodynamic noise—do not appear to be sufficiently considered by those who regard the aural method as being generally reliable. The engine beat, or resonance, which figures so largely in the correspondence to which I have referred, is common to practically all types of twin-engine aircraft and is to some extent controllable by the pilot.

The question may be asked: "If it is a fact that experienced spotters can recognise many types of *British* aircraft by their characteristic sound alone, why should there be greater difficulty or less certainty in the recognition of *hostile* types?" The answer, surprisingly enough, is lack of practice!

We may listen to the sound of hostile planes droning overhead night after night yet, if we are unable to verify by sight, or in some other manner, the opinions which we tentatively form at the time, they remain merely opinions, held without firm conviction. There is nevertheless little chance of them being successfully challenged. Thus we find that a night raider, flying above cloud and screened from searchlights, may be variously reported as a Dornier, a Heinkel or a Junkers. When a fortunate burst brings it down and the charred remains are examined, it probably proves to be a Messerschmitt 110!

Daylight raids carried out by formations of single-engine fighters and twin-engine bombers flying at great heights provide no better opportunity for singling out and impressing upon the memory the note of any individual hostile type. "Tip and run" raids accompanied by low altitude bombing and dive bombing, are most frequently carried out under conditions of general or local low visibility.

If we consider the unfavourable musical conditions of a raid—the prelude of the sirens, the bass accompaniment of the barrage, the dominating theme of large formations and the incidental music contributed by interceptor fighters—we can readily appreciate that comparatively few spotters have had repeated opportunities of familiarising themselves with the individual and characteristic notes of many different types of hostile aircraft.

Photograph : Charles E. Brown.

1. Vickers Supermarine " Spitfire " single-seat fighters.
Rolls-Royce " Merlin " engine.

Photograph : " The Aeroplane."

2. Heinkel 113 single-seat fighter. Daimler-Benz engine.

Photograph : " The Aeroplane."

3. Hawker " Hurricane " single-seat fighters.   Rolls-Royce
" Merlin " engine.

Photograph : " The Aeroplane."

4. Boulton Paul " Defiant " two-seat fighter.   Rolls-Royce
" Merlin " engine.

Photograph : " Flight."

5. Blackburn " Skua " two-seat fighter and dive-bomber
of the Fleet Air Arm.   Bristol " Perseus " engine.

Photograph : Phillips and Powis Aircraft, Ltd.

6. Miles " Magister " initial trainer.   Gipsy " Major "
engine.

Photograph : Phillips and Powis Aircraft, Ltd.

7. Miles " Master " advanced trainer. Rolls-Royce " Kestrel " engine.

Photograph : " The Aeroplane.'

8. A parade of Heinkel IIIK MkV twin-engine bombers on the occasion of Hitler's birthday. Junkers " Jumo " engines.

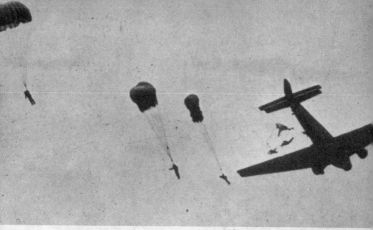

Photograph : " The Aeroplane."

9. German parachute-troops leaving the three-motor Junkers 52
(B.M.W. engines). Note the early opening of the parachutes,
effected by means of a special rip-cord which the para-
chutist hooks on to the side of the fuselage before jumping.

Photograph : " The Aeroplane."

10. The Messerschmitt " Jaguar," reconnaissance bomber version
of the Me.110 twin-engine fighter. Daimler-Benz engines.

Photograph : '' *The Aeroplane.*''

11. Junkers 86 twin-engine air-liners of South African Airways, now serving with the South African Air Force.

Photograph : '' *Jane's Aircraft*

12. Junkers 90 four-engine troop transport.

Photograph : " The Aeroplane."

13. Junkers 88 twin-engine dive-bomber. Junkers " Jumo "
engines. Note the external bomb-racks and the
" venetian blind " dive brakes suspended from the wings.

Photograph . " Flight."

14. Bristol " Blenheim " Mk IV twin-engine medium
bomber. Bristol " Mercury " engines.

Photograph : " The Aeroplane."

15. Bristol " Beaufort " bomber, reconnaissance and torpedo plane. Two Bristol " Taurus " engines.

Photograph : Charles E. Brown.

16. Vickers " Wellington " twin-engine long-range heavy bombers (MkIA). Bristol " Pegasus " engines.

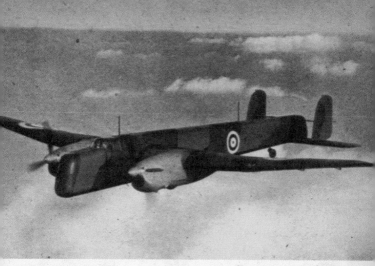

Photograph : " The Aeroplane."

17. Armstrong-Whitworth " Whitley " long-range heavy bomber. Note twin fins (braced) and rudders mounted on top of the tailplane.

Photograph : " The Aeroplane."

18. Handley Page " Hampden " twin engine long-range bomber. Bristol " Pegasus " engines.

Photograph . "The Aeroplane."

19. A pioneer of "flying wing" construction the Junkers G.38 "v
Hindenburg," a frequent visitor to Croydon several years ago. Th
type is now used as a troop transport. Four Junkers L88A engine

Photograph : Charles E. Brown.

20. Westland "Lysander" army co-operation and reconnaissance
monoplane. Bristol "Mercury" or "Perseus" engine.

Photograph : " The Aeroplane."

21. De Havilland " Flamingo," or R.A.F. " Hertfordshire "
twin-engine communications and transport 'plane.
Bristol " Perseus " engines.

Photograph : " The Aeroplane."

22. Dornier 215 long-range heavy bombers. Photo shows
the type fitted with radial engines. Compare with
silhouettes on page 117 showing do. 215 fitted with
liquid-cooled in-line engines.

23. Handley Page "Harrow" twin-engine bomber or
   troop transport. Bristol "Pegasus" engines.

24 A Vickers Supermarine "Walrus" amphibian flying
   boat is launched by catapult from the mother ship.
   One Bristol "Pegasus" engine.

Photograph : " Jane's Aircraft."

25. Blohm and Voss Ha. 139 four-engine float seaplane.
Communication, troop transport and mine laying.
Junkers " Jumo " Diesel engines.

Photograph : " Jane's Aircraft."

26. Dornier .18 twin-engine reconnaissance or bomber
flying boat. Two Junkers " Jumo " Diesel engines
mounted in tandem.

Photograph : " Jane's Aircraft."

27. Consolidated Model 28-5 or PBY 5, photographed over San Diego, California, prior to its departure for Felixstowe. Two Pratt and Whitney Twin-Wasp engines.

28. Dornier 24 three-engine reconnaissance flying boat. Note the stub wing or sponson. B.M.W. engines.

Photograph : Beken & Son.

29. Saro "Lerwick" general purpose flying boat of the
Coastal Command. Two Bristol "Hercules" engines.

Photograph : "The Aeroplane."

30. Short "Sunderland" flying boat of the Coastal
Command. Four Bristol "Pegasus" engines.

Photograph : Beken & Son.

31. The float-seaplane version of the Fairey " Swordfish " which, like
     its successor, the Fairey " Albacore," is specially designed as a
     torpedo plane.   This type was responsible for the crippling
     of the Italian Navy, at Taranto and off Sardinia.   The
     torpedo is carried between the undercarriage struts.   A
     wheel undercarriage is fitted for operation from the
     decks of aircraft carriers.   Bristol " Pegasus " engine.

Photograph : The Fairey Aviation Co., Ltd.

32. Fairey " Albacore." A later type designed for the same functions as
     the famous " Swordfish," and fitted with the more powerful Bristol
     " Taurus " engine.

AIRCRAFT SILHOUETTES

With descriptive notes by the Author

33

B

AIRCRAFT SILHOUETTES

SECTION I

LOW-WING MONOPLANES

35

VICKERS-SUPERMARINE "SPITFIRE"

ACCORDING to figures officially released, the fastest single-seat fighter in service with the R.A.F., having a maximum speed of 367 m.p.h. With four Browning guns in each wing, the " Spitfire " has a total rate of fire of 9,600 rounds per minute. Its superlative qualities as an interceptor fighter are only matched by the skill and determination of R.A.F. pilots. Spitfire and Hurricane squadrons have between them destroyed Goering's hope of attaining aerial supremacy over Britain. Power unit is the famous Rolls-Royce Merlin liquid-cooled engine developing more than 1,000 h.p.

A modified " Spitfire " with more powerful " Merlin " engine and " clipped," square-cut wing-tips, is now coming into service. The new " Spitfire," Mk III, is considerably faster than the standard type, and its armament includes cannon.

Principal Structural Features

Low-wing monoplane; wings of elliptical plan with pointed tips and full dihedral. Single in-line engine; single fin and rudder; finely streamlined fuselage. Retractable undercarriage.

Special Recognition Points

Fuselage is slimmer and less hump-backed than the "Hurricane." The rounded fin and rudder is smaller and narrower than that of the Hurricane. Elliptical plan view of wings and tail-plane is distinctive. Wheels retract outwards.

Head-on view: Note full dihedral and radiator under the starboard wing. The "Hurricane" has very slight dihedral and the radiator is centred under the fuselage.

SPITFIRE Mk I (Merlin)
Fighter
Span 36' 10" Length 29' 11" Height 9' 3"

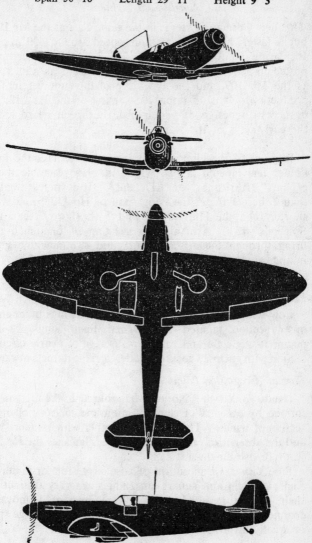

HEINKEL 113

Single-Seat Fighter

THIS new German fighter is in the same class as the Me 109, but is faster, having a maximum speed around 400 m.p.h. Increasing numbers of the He 113 have lately been reported in action, although it is by no means as numerous as the Me 109, and the type is probably not yet in full production. It is an improved version of the He 112, an unsuccessful design of which little has been heard since the early days of the war.

In place of the elliptical wings of the He 112, the new fighter has tapered wings, which in plan resemble those of the " Hurricane " or " Defiant." It is much smaller than either of these, the wing span of He 113 being 9 ft. shorter than the Hurricane's and 5 ft. shorter than the Spitfire's span. Armament, consisting of one shell-gun firing through the airscrew hub, and two machine guns in the wings, is inferior to that of the well-tried R.A.F. single-seat fighters.

Principal Structural Features

Low-wing monoplane, centre section of wings untapered, outer section tapered to rounded tips. Single in-line engine ; single fin and rudder ; fuselage of nearly circular section with enclosed cockpit; undercarriage retracts inwards.

Special Recognition Points

Head-on View : Notice the inverted " gull wing " formed by *anhedral* of centre section and *dihedral* of outer section of wings. This feature, together with smaller span and the absence of radiator, clearly distinguishes the He 113 from British single-seat fighters.

Side View : Clean outline of nose suggests a large calibre shell ; tall fin and square-cut rudder are very distinctive, their outline resembling the closed jaws of a movable spanner. In plan view the tapered tailplane of large span is equally distinctive.

HEINKEL 113
Single–Seat Fighter
Span 30′ 11″   Length 26′ 7″   Height 8′ 2″

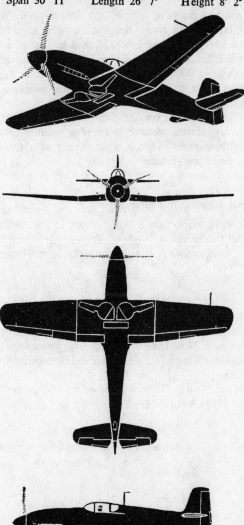

HAWKER "HURRICANE"

THIS most successful single-seat interceptor fighter is slightly larger than the "Spitfire" and not quite so fast, having a maximum speed of 335 m.p.h. Like the "Spitfire," it is fitted with Rolls-Royce Merlin engine, developing more than 1,000 h.p. "Hurricane" and "Spitfire" squadrons have together beaten off innumerable massed raids against Britain, and although heavily outnumbered by escorting fighters, have brilliantly sustained the R.A.F. tradition of fearless attack. Their armament consists of four machine-guns in each wing, firing at a total rate of 9,600 rounds per minute.

Principal Structural Features

Low-wing monoplane ; wings taper to rounded tips with very slight dihedral. Single in-line engine. Single fin and rudder ; streamline fuselage ; retractable undercarriage.

Special Recognition Points

Plan view : Uniformly tapered wing and tail-plane, both having well-rounded tips. Wheels retract inwards.

Side view : Note the hump-backed appearance of fuselage and large well-rounded fin and rudder continued beneath the fuselage.

Head-on view : Negligible dihedral and centrally placed radiator distinguish "Hurricane" from "Spitfire."

HURRICANE (Merlin)
Single–Seat Fighter
Span 40′ 0″   Length 31′ 5″   Height 11′ 3″

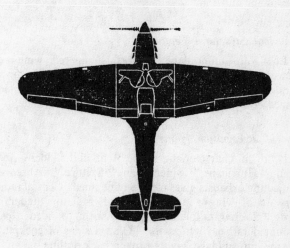

MESSERSCHMITT 109

Single-seat Fighter

THE brunt of the short-range bomber escort work is borne by the Messerschmitt 109 single-seat fighter. Originally armed with four machine-guns and one 23 mm. cannon, firing through the air-screw hub, later types are fitted with two machine-guns and a small cannon in each wing. The combined fire power of this armament is inferior to that of R.A.F. fighters. Owing to the heavy casualties sustained by Nazi bombers, the Me 109 is on occasion used as a light bomber. With maximum speed of 354 m.p.h., the Me 109 fighter, after releasing its bombs, may more easily evade the attentions of the R.A.F. The power unit is now the Daimler-Benz 601 liquid-cooled engine of 1,150 h.p. (Me 109E). Silhouette shows Me 109 with D.B. 600 engine of 1,050 h.p.

Principal Structural Features

Low-wing monoplane, uniformly tapered wings with almost square-cut tips and full dihedral. Single fin and rudder, streamline fuselage of oval section with enclosed glazed cockpit. Outwardly retracting undercarriage.

Special Recognition Points

Note the characteristic shape of fin and rudder—smaller than " Hurricane," wider than " Spitfire." Absence of projecting exhausts gives clean engine line. Central radiator forward of wings ; additional small radiators under each wing. *Braced* tailplane, tapered with rounded tips, is mounted rather high on fin. Glazed sides of cockpit bite deeply into fuselage, giving broken back outline.

MESSERSCHMITT 109 (D.B. 600)
Single–Seat Fighter
Span 32′ 5″   Length 28′ 3″   Height 8′ 4″

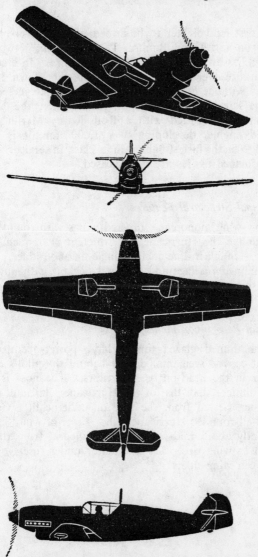

BOULTON PAUL "DEFIANT"

Fighter

THE first land fighter to be armed with a power-operated four-gun turret, the Boulton Paul "Defiant" two-seater fighter has an unusually wide field of fire. In a surprise appearance over Dunkirk, 12 Defiants shot down 38 Nazi planes without loss to themselves. The bag included 16 of the latest German twin-engined fighter, the Messerschmitt 110. Fitted with a Rolls-Royce Merlin liquid-cooled engine, developing over 1,000 h.p., it is understood to be the fastest fighter, in its class, in service. Actual performance figures are not released.

Principal Structural Features

Low-wing monoplane, tapered wings with rounded tips, not unlike the Hurricane, for which it is frequently mistaken. Single in-line engine, single fin and rudder. Finely streamlined fuselage and enclosed cockpit with gun-turret amidships. Undercarriage retracts inwards.

Special Recognition Points

The domed glazed top of large power-operated gun-turret can be seen immediately behind the pilot's cockpit, either in the head-on or side views. The nose is longer and slimmer than that of the Hurricane; tail unit angular whether viewed from the side or underneath. Compare the well-rounded Hurricane tail. Taper of wings increases abruptly about mid-way. Slight dihedral from the same point to wing tips. Large radiator under fuselage centre, between wing fillets.

DEFIANT (Merlin)
Fighter
Span 39′ 4″   Length 35′ 4″   Height 12′ 2″

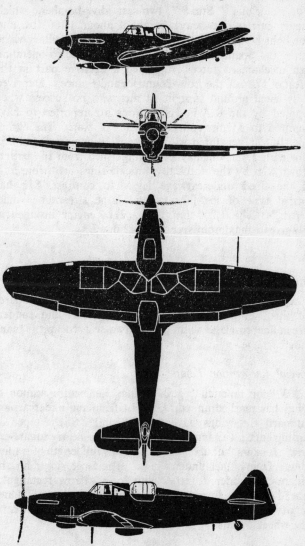

JUNKERS 87

THE notorious "Stuka" two-seat dive-bomber, which usually carries one heavy bomb of about 1,100 lbs. and four light bombs of 110 lbs. each, proved its military value during the Spanish Civil War. Used in close co-operation with mechanised forces, it played a decisive part in the defeat of Poland, the Low Countries and France. Deprived of its usual ground support, it met with no success when opposed by the R.A.F. Squadrons are reported to have migrated to Mediterranean theatres of war. The earlier type, Ju 87a, was fitted with a Jumo 210 engine of 640 h.p. This earlier version may be distinguished from the better-known 87b by the unusually wide fairings or "trousers" on the fixed undercarriage legs. In contrast, 87b has normal type of leg fairings and large streamline wheel "spats." The 1,200 h.p. Jumo 211A engine installed in 87b gives a maximum speed of 242 m.p.h.

Principal Structural Features

Low-wing monoplane with tapered wings and square-cut tips. Single in-line engine; single fin and rudder. Streamline fuselage with glazed two-seat cockpit. Fixed undercarriage.

Special Recognition Points

" W " or inverted " gull " wings, i.e. centre section of wings has marked anhedral, whilst from the undercarriage outboard the wings have full dihedral. Slight taper on leading edge; full taper on trailing edge; nearly square-cut tips. Junkers " double wing " or flaps full length of trailing edge. Dive brakes under wings. The large single fin and square-cut rudder, together with long narrow rectangular braced tailplane, form a most characteristic tail unit. Large radiator is centrally placed under the engines. Large stream-line wheel " spats."

JUNKERS 87B
Dive Bomber
Span 45' 3"   **Length 35' 4"**   **Height 12' 8"**

BLACKBURN "SKUA"

Two-seat Dive Bomber of the Fleet Air Arm

THE "Skua" fighter and dive bomber is the first *monoplane* operated by the Fleet Air Arm from aircraft carriers. It is fitted with deck-landing arrestor, wings which fold for stowage, and is adapted for launching by catapult. The Bristol Perseus sleeve-valve radial engine, developing over 900 h.p., gives the "Skua" a maximum speed of 225 m.p.h. The specially designed water-tight fuselage enables the machine to remain afloat for some time after an emergency landing. The "Skua" is frequently in the news in connection with dive-bombing raids upon the channel invasion ports and coastal aerodromes.

Principal Structural Features

Low-wing monoplane, tapered wings with rounded tips and moderate dihedral; single radial engine; single fin and rudder. Fuselage of circular section. Special flaps control diving speed. Retractable undercarriage.

Special Recognition Points

Wings with moderate dihedral throughout most of their span, are sharply upswept at the tips. Wing taper is more marked on the trailing edge. Long wing fillets integral with the fuselage. Tall rounded fin and rudder of characteristic shape is set well forward of the tailplane; the fin is continued underneath the tail; long narrow tailplane with very slight taper and rounded tips. Distinctive coupé type two-seat cockpit with large glazed panels between wide pillars.

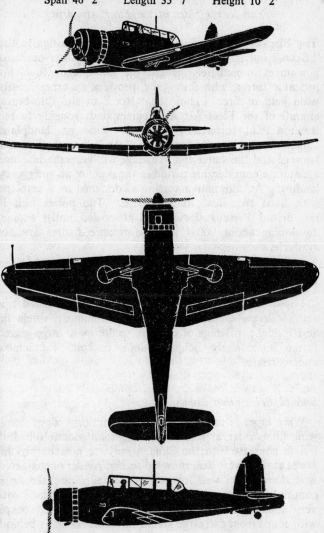

BLACKBURN "ROC"

Two-seat Fighter of the Fleet Air Arm

THE Blackburn " Roc " is similar in general design to the
" Skua," but is fitted with a Boulton Paul power-operated
gun-turret immediately behind the pilot's cockpit. This
rotatable turret, with four guns, provides an exceptionally
wide field of fire. Thus the " Roc " in the ship-borne
aircraft of the Fleet Air Arm corresponds roughly to the
Boulton Paul turretted " Defiant " amongst landplane
fighters. Like the " Skua," the " Roc's " wings fold for
stowage and the water-tight fuselage will keep the machine
afloat for a considerable period in the event of an emergency
landing. An alternative version is designed as a seaplane
with fixed twin-float undercarriage. The power unit is
the Bristol Perseus sleeve-valve air-cooled radial engine,
developing about 900 h.p. Performance figures are not
available.

Principal Structural Features

Low-wing monoplane, tapered wings with rounded tips
and moderate dihedral ; single radial engine ; single fin
and rudder ; fuselage of circular section with large glazed
turret immediately behind pilot's cockpit. Retractable
undercarriage.

Special Recognition Points

Wing taper is more marked on the trailing edge ; long
wing fillets integral with the fuselage ; moderate dihedral,
but in contrast with the Skua, wings are not sharply upswept at the tips. Tall rounded fin and rudder of characteristic shape is set well forward of the tailplane ; the fin is
continued underneath the tail ; long narrow tailplane with
very slight taper and rounded tips. Distinctive cockpit
with coupé front and large glazed turret immediately behind.

50

ROC. I (Perseus)
Two–Seater Fighter (F.A.A.)
Span 46′ 0″   Length 35′ 7″   Height 14′ 2″

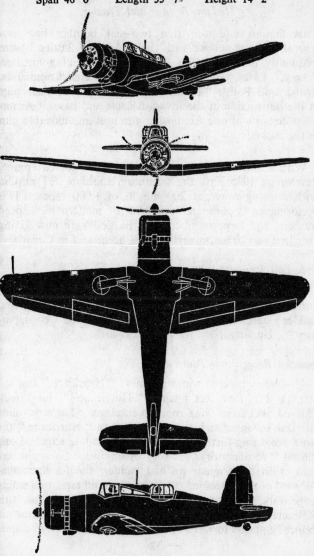

FAIREY "BATTLE"

Medium Bomber and Trainer

THIS famous and well-tried two-seat bomber has seen several years of service with the R.A.F. "Battles" were frequently in action with the advanced striking force in France. Later, with the Bomber and Coastal Commands, British and Polish "Battle" squadrons played their part in the destruction of the invasion fleets and bases. Armament consists of one fixed wing gun and one movable gun in the cockpit.

With a single Rolls-Royce Merlin liquid-cooled engine, developing 1035 h.p., the maximum speed is 257 m.p.h., with cruising range, at 200 m.p.h., of 1,000 miles. This performance is comparable to that of modern high-speed trainers, and large numbers of "Battles" are now giving excellent service as trainers both at home and in Canada.

Principal Structural Features

Low-wing monoplane, tapered wings with rounded tips and slight dihedral; single in-line engine; single fin and rudder; streamline fuselage with large glazed "conservatory." Undercarriage retracts backwards.

Special Recognition Points

Uniformly tapered wings resemble "Hurricane," but the span is fifty-four feet against "Hurricane's" forty feet. Curved fillet from wing roots to fuselage. The streamline fuselage is longer and more slender than "Hurricane," the nose projecting further forward of the leading edge. Long glazed "conservatory" is very distinctive. So is the tail unit, with tall angular fin and rudder, the fin somewhat forward of the tailplane. Tailplane has full taper on leading edge only, rounded tips and is mounted low on fuselage. Retracted wheels are partially exposed. Radiator is centrally placed forward of leading edge.

BATTLE I (Merlin)
Medium Bomber and Trainer
Span 54' 0"   Length 42' 4"   Height 15' 0"

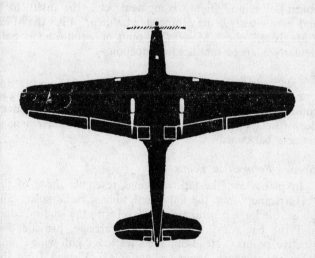

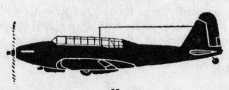

MILES " MASTER I "

Trainer

A MODIFIED version of the 295 m.p.h. Miles " Kestrel "
monoplane trainer produced by Phillips & Powis in 1937,
considerable quantities of the " Master I " advanced trainer
came into service in the R.A.F. in 1939.

Fitted with a single Rolls-Royce " Kestrel XXX " liquid-
cooled in-line engine, developing 715 h.p., the " Master "
cruises at 225 m.p.h., and has a top speed of 264 m.p.h.,
i.e. faster than the " Gladiator." Extremely manœuvrable,
the flying and handling qualities of this advanced trainer
correspond very closely to those of the " Hurricane " and
" Spitfire." The large enclosed cockpit is fitted with dual
control, " blind " flying equipment, etc., the instructor's
and pilot's seats being arranged in tandem. Like the Miles
" Magister," the " Master " is built of wood, and is particularly adapted for rapid production.

Principal Structural Features.

Low-wing monoplane, inverted " gull-wing," tapering to
rounded tips. Single in-line engine ; single fin and rudder ;
deep fuselage with glazed two-seat cockpit ; undercarriage
retracts backwards.

Special Recognition Points

In plan view, the tapered wings resemble those of the
" Hurricane," but the untapered, almost rectangular, tailplane, the large central radiator level with the leading edge,
and the backward retracting undercarriage, provide distinctive points. Head-on, the inverted " gull-wing " and
large radiator are easily recognisable. Viewed from the
side, the unusually large fin and rudder with well-rounded
top and wide base, together with deep glazed coupé cockpit,
deep radiator forward, form a characteristic silhouette.
Tailplane is mounted on top of the fuselage forward of
the rudder.

MASTER I (Kestrel)
Trainer
Span 39' 0"   Length 30' 8"   Height 11' 6"

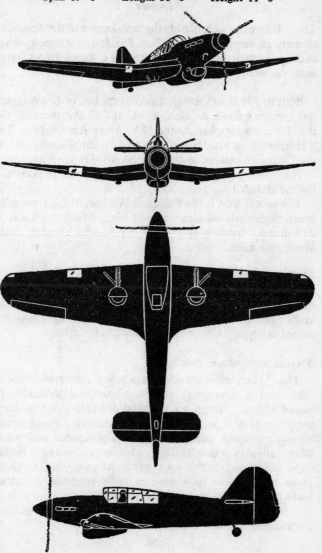

NORTH AMERICAN "HARVARD"

Trainer

THE "Harvard" is probably the best-known of the American trainers in service with the R.A.F. It is extremely noisy and can usually be recognised from a distance by its harsh note, caused by the high tip-speed of the airscrew.

Built by the North American Aviation Inc. of Los Angeles, the type is known as N.A.-16-3, and is the same as the B.C.1 trainer supplied to the U.S. Army Air Corps. The "Harvard" is also being delivered in large quantities to the Canadian centres of the Empire Air Training Scheme.

The "Wirraway" is a modified version built in Australia for the R.A.A.F.

The power unit is the Pratt and Whitney Wasp air-cooled radial engine, developing 550–600 h.p. Maximum speed is 210 m.p.h., cruising speed 196 m.p.h., and cruising range about 900 miles.

Principal Structural Features

Low-wing monoplane wings tapered on leading edge only, with rounded tips ; single radial engine ; single fin and rudder ; fuselage of circular section with long two-seat glazed cockpit. Undercarriage retracts inwards.

Special Recognition Points

The "Harvard" sounds like a noisy two-stroke motor-cycle and is frequently recognised without difficulty by sound alone. Wings are equally distinctive. The short centre section is without taper or dihedral. From centre section outboard, leading edge is fully tapered and wings have full dihedral. Trailing edge is untapered. Radial engine gives a stubby appearance to nose and fuselage. High tailplane is fully tapered with rounded elevators. Note the long two-seat "conservatory."

Mk. II has nearly square-cut wing-tips and angular—instead of rounded—rudder.

HARVARD I (Wasp)
Trainer
Span 43' 0"   Length 27' 9¼"   Height 11' 8½"

57

MILES "MAGISTER I"

Trainer

DEVELOPED from the successful Miles "Hawk" series of light low-wing touring monoplanes, the "Magister" has been in service with the R.A.F. since 1936. It is the only monoplane used for *initial* training. Monoplanes of the "Master," "Harvard" and "Battle" types, capable of speeds exceeding 200 m.p.h., are used as advanced trainers.

Since all modern designs of fighters and bombers are of monoplane type, primary training in monoplanes is likely to become more general.

Like the "Tiger Moth," the "Magister" is fitted with the 130 h.p. Gipsy Major inverted air-cooled in-line engine, giving a maximum speed of 142 m.p.h. and cruising speed around 130 m.p.h. The stalling speed of 45 m.p.h. is only slightly higher than that of standard biplane trainers.

The Cirrus "Major 150" in-line inverted air-cooled engine, developing 150 h.p., is an alternative power unit.

Principal Structural Features

Low-wing monoplane, tapered wings with rounded tips and full dihedral. Single in-line engine; single fin and rudder; fuselage of roughly oval section with two-seat open cockpits, in tandem. Fixed undercarriage.

Special Recognition Points

Wings have very slight taper and wide rounded tips. Full dihedral from undercarriage legs to wing tips. Streamline fillets from trailing edge to fuselage. Tailplane, mounted on top of fuselage, forward of rudder, is almost rectangular. Fin and rudder maintain the general angular appearance of the "Magister's" tail unit. Single-strutted (cantilever) vertical legs of fixed undercarriage are placed wide apart; wheels have small streamline "spats."

MAGISTER I (Gipsy Major)
Training
Span 33' 10"   Length 25' 3"   Height 9' 9"

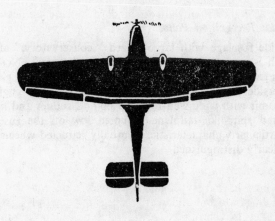

AVRO "ANSON"

In production for the R.A.F. for several years, the Avro "Anson" is still giving excellent service on coastal reconnaissance work. Although its top speed is only 188 m.p.h. and cruising speed 158, it has successfully dealt with attacking fighters on numerous occasions. Powered by two 350 h.p. Armstrong-Siddeley "Cheetah" engines, "Ansons" are extensively used as twin-engined trainers.

Principal Structural Features

Low-wing monoplane, uniformly tapered wings with rounded tips and moderate dihedral. Twin radial engines mounted on their centre lines. Wide fuselage forward, slender tail, single fin and rudder. Wheels partially retract into engine nacelles.

Special Recognition Points

Wide fuselage with large glazed "conservatory," aft of which is mounted a glazed rotatable gun-turret. Nose of fuselage projects slightly forward of engines, with glazed underside. Note the fluted cowling of Cheetah engines. Tail unit with wide well-rounded fin and rudder and finely tapered spur-like tailplane mounted low on the fuselage is particularly characteristic. Partially retracted wheels can be clearly distinguished.

ANSON (2-Cheetah IX)
Reconnaissance and Training
Span 56′ 6″   Length 42′ 3″   Height 13′ 0″

HEINKEL 111 K Mk V

Long-range Heavy Bomber

IN production since 1935, when with two 660 h.p. B.M.W.
engines its maximum speed was only 211 m.p.h., the design
of the Heinkel 111 K has been frequently modified. The
" K " for " Kreig," denotes the military version of the
well-known Heinkel 111 civil air-liner. The silhouettes
show the current design, Mk V. Earlier types which had
wings of elliptical plan and inadequate armament proved
easy meat for R.A.F. fighters. Mk V has fared little
better. With two Daimler-Benz liquid-cooled engines of
1,150 h.p., the maximum speed is 274 m.p.h., and cruising
speed 230 m.p.h. Specimens of a later series of Mk V
fitted with 1,200 h.p. Junkers Jumo engines have also been
shot down.

Principal Structural Features

Low wing monoplane with tapered wings, rounded tips
and full dihedral. Two in-line engines, nacelles slightly
under-slung with radiator beneath. Single fin and rudder.
Slender streamline fuselage of circular section. Undercarriage retracts into nacelles.

Special Recognition Points

Earlier versions have elliptical wing plan. Mk V has
fully tapered wings as shown in silhouettes, with rounded
tips and full dihedral. The taper is more marked on
leading edge. The trailing edge is swept *forward* near
the wing roots. This " bite " is characteristic of many
Heinkel designs. Glazed bomb-aiming nose projects as
far forward as engines. (Earlier versions are distinguished
by long slender nose projecting forward of engines.) Under-
gun emplacement just aft of wings. Small glazed " pimple "
screens the upper gun position. Single tall rounded fin
and rudder with rudder cut away at its base. The tailplane retains the characteristic elliptical plan of the earlier
versions.

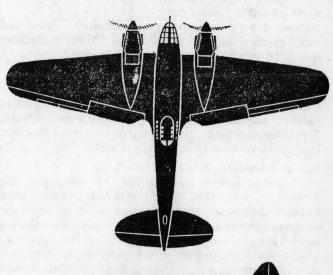

AIRSPEED " OXFORD "

Trainer

BEFORE taking over the controls of a high-speed twin-engine bomber or fighter, the pilot and crew must be thoroughly trained in the handling of a two-motor aircraft in navigation, photography, gunnery, etc. The " Oxford," specially designed for that purpose, is the standard twin-engine advanced trainer of the Royal Air Force. Large numbers of them are in service in Canada.

Normally carrying a crew of three, the " Oxford " is fitted with dual control, and modifications of equipment provide for training in bomb-aiming, gunnery, aerial photography, radio communication, blind flying and navigation. The drawings show the version of the " Oxford " adapted for gunnery training and fitted with the Armstrong-Whitworth rotatable gun-turret.

Powered with two 375 h.p. " Cheetah X " air-cooled radial engines, the maximum speed is 190 m.p.h., cruising speed 166 m.p.h., and stalling speed 56 m.p.h.

Principal Structural Features

Low-wing monoplane, tapered wings with rounded tips and full dihedral ; two radial engines ; single fin and rudder ; slab-sided fuselage with control cabin forward. Some versions have rear gun-turret on top of fuselage. Undercarriage retracts into engine nacelles.

Special Recognition Points

In general design the " Oxford " is not unlike the " Anson." Seen head-on, the dihedral is much more marked ; engine nacelles are mounted two-thirds above the wings, and the tail unit is carried higher. In plan, the sharply tapered wings, the engine nacelles projecting aft of the trailing edge, and the rounded tailplane are distinctive. Side view shows the characteristic angular " Oxford " fin and rudder and smaller glazed cabin. The " Cheetah X " has plain cowling in contrast to the fluted cowling of the Anson's " Cheetah I X." The undercarriage wheels are partially exposed when retracted.

OXFORD (2–Cheetah)
Trainer
Span 53′ 4″   Length 34′ 6″   Height 11′ 1¼″

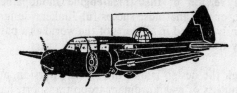

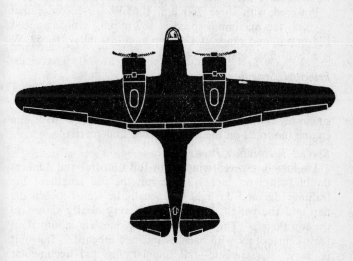

JUNKERS 52

THE civil version of this three-engine monoplane, type Ju 52/3M, one of the most successful Junkers designs, has been extensively used in all parts of the world as a passenger and heavy transport plane for nearly ten years.

Although the design is old, the military version, adapted for parachutists or as an ordinary troop transport, has been built in large quantities. It played a very important rôle in the invasions of Norway and the Low Countries.

The normal load of Ju 52 is about fourteen fully equipped parachutists, or as a short distance heavy transport it may carry more than two tons of arms and equipment. There is a machine-gun position on top of the fuselage well aft, and some versions have the " dustbin " type of under-gun position.

Powered with three 760 h.p. B.M.W. air-cooled radial engines, the maximum speed is 189 m.p.h., cruising speed 175 m.p.h. and range at 149 m.p.h., 1,000 miles. Ju 52/W is a twin-float seaplane version.

Principal Structural Features

Low-wing monoplane, tapered wings, with full dihedral, narrow, almost square-cut, tips. Three radial engines ; single fin and rudder ; large slab-sided fuselage with one engine mounted on the nose. Fixed undercarriage.

Special Recognition Points

Uniformly tapered wings with full dihedral and Junkers double-wings or flaps. These run the full length of the trailing edge and daylight can usually be seen between the flap and the wing. This feature is very clearly shown in the top sketch. The two outboard engines are mounted on their centre-lines with nacelles inclined inboard. Tail unit is very characteristic—tall angular fin and rectangular rudder with unusually long and narrow braced tailplane. The elevators are of Junkers double-wing type and project beyond the tips of the tailplane. External surfaces of fuselage, wings, etc., are constructed in corrugated sheet metal. Undercarriage is low and compact, with " spatted " wheels.

JUNKERS 52
Parachute/Troop Transport
Span 96' 0" Length 62' 0" Height 18' 0"

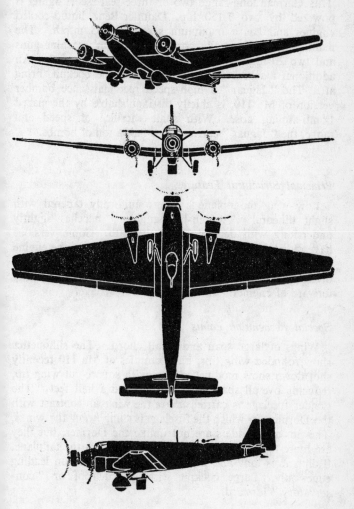

MESSERSCHMITT 110 AND "JAGUAR"

THIS German long-range two or three-seat escort fighter is powered by two 1,150 h.p. Daimler-Benz liquid-cooled engines and has a maximum speed of 365 m.p.h. The main armament, usually consisting of four machine-guns and two 20 mm. shell guns, is installed in the nose. An additional machine-gun is mounted in the cockpit firing aft. The "Jaguar" a high-speed reconnaissance bomber version of Me 110, is chiefly distinguishable by the glazed bomb-aiming nose. With some sacrifice of speed and range, the "Jaguar" carries up to half a ton of bombs.

Principal Structural Features

Low-wing monoplane; wings uniformly tapered with slight dihedral. Two in-line engines; nacelles slightly underslung with deep radiators beneath. Some versions have radiators under each wing, just outboard of the engine nacelles. Twin fins and rudders mounted at extreme tips of tailplane. Streamline nose of fuselage projects slightly forward of engines. Retractable undercarriage.

Special Recognition Points

Wings of large span and small chord. The silhouettes show rounded wing tips, but examples of Me 110 recently shot down show modified design with square-cut wing tip, reducing overall span by about one and a half feet. The slender fuselage is carried *above* the wings in contrast with the Dornier, in which the fuselage is slung *below* the wings. The fins and rudders are not unlike the Dornier, but they are more rounded and are mounted lower on the tailplane. Tailplane is long and narrow with slight taper on leading edge only. Large cockpit with glazed roof or "conservatory" forward.

MESSERSCHMITT 110
Twin-Engine Fighter
Span 53' 4"   Length 40' 6"   Height 12' 0"

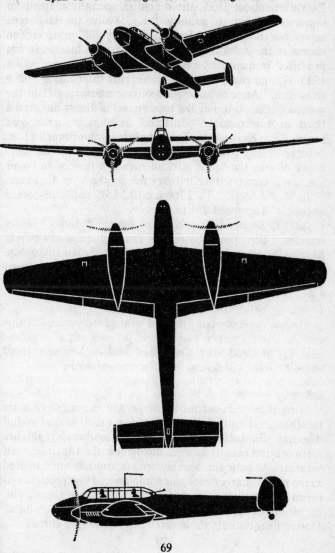

JUNKERS 86 and 86K

PRODUCED about 1935, the design is specially adapted for rapid conversion to military use. Whilst the civil type serves as a troop-carrier, Ju 86K, the fully militarised version shewn in these drawings, is designed as a bomber. It was produced in quantities for the Luftwaffe during the period 1935-37, and played a considerable part in crushing Polish resistance. Armament consists of one machine-gun in the nose, another on top of the fuselage aft of the wings, and a third in a retractable " dustbin " or rotatable under-gun turret. The Swedish Air Force includes a number of Ju 86K bombers fitted with Bristol radial engines. On the outbreak of war, the South African Airway's fleet of Ju 86 air liners was converted for military use by the S.A. Air Force.

Ju 86 *Air Liner*. Two 760 h.p. B.M.W. radial air-cooled engines. Top speed 233 m.p.h.

Ju 86 *K Bomber*. Two 700 h.p. Junkers " Jumo " Diesel engines. Top speed 224 m.p.h., cruising speed 174 m.p.h. Maximum range exceeds 1,500 miles. Or two 880 h.p. B.M.W. air-cooled radial engines ; maximum speed 238 m.p.h., cruising speed 214 m.p.h.

Principal Structural Features

Low-wing monoplane, tapered wings with square-cut tips and dihedral ; either two in-line or two radial engines ; twin fins and rudders ; fuselage of oval section with small control cabin ; undercarriage retracts outwards.

Special Recognition Points

Wing plan of characteristic Junkers form ; angle of taper increasing abruptly mid-way along the wings ; full dihedral. Junkers double-wing flaps, showing daylight, are fitted. Deep narrow nacelles distinguish the Diesel-engined version. Angular fins and square-cut rudders are mounted at the tips of nearly rectangular tailplane. Nose projects well forward of engines. Nose of bomber version is glazed, with projecting gun-turret. Rear gunner's cockpit is partly enclosed. Dotted lines indicate the lowered position of gun-turret.

JUNKERS 86K
Bomber
Span 73' 8"   Length 57' 4"   Height 15' 7"

JUNKERS 89 and 90

Ju 89 is the military version of the Ju 90, a forty-passenger four-engine air liner in regular service since 1937 on the principal Lufthansa European air lines. The civil version, shown in these drawings, now serves chiefly as a troop carrier and heavy transport plane. Crew and fuel included, it is capable of carrying a load of nearly seven tons.

Ju 90 is fitted with four 880 h.p. B.M.W. radial air-cooled engines giving a maximum speed of 217 m.p.h., cruising speed of 198 m.p.h. and range of 1,300 miles.

Ju 89, the bomber version, is fitted with four 1,200 h.p. Junkers " Jumo " liquid-cooled engines. It is believed to have a maximum speed of 225 m.p.h. and cruising speed around 200 m.p.h. There is a glazed bomb-aiming turret in the nose, a tail gun-turret and additional gun positions in the fuselage. Apart from these modifications, the general appearance of the civil and military types is the same.

Principal Structural Features

Low-wing monoplane, wings sharply tapered on leading edge to narrow tips, full dihedral. Ju 89 : four in-line engines. Ju 90 : four radial engines. Twin fins and rudders ; large fuselage of roughly oval section.

Special Recognition Points

This wing plan is most characteristic, having very sharp taper on the leading edge, narrow tips swept inboard, and slightly back-swept trailing edge. Junkers " double-wing " flaps—between which daylight can usually be seen—are fitted. Dihedral is more marked from inboard engines to tips. Twin fins and rudders of distinctive Junkers design are attached close to tailplane tips. Tapered tailplane is mounted on top of the fuselage forward of the streamline tail. Fuselage is deep and somewhat slab-sided forward, the streamline nose projecting far forward of the engines. Fairings enclosing the retracted wheels can be distinguished under the inner nacelles.

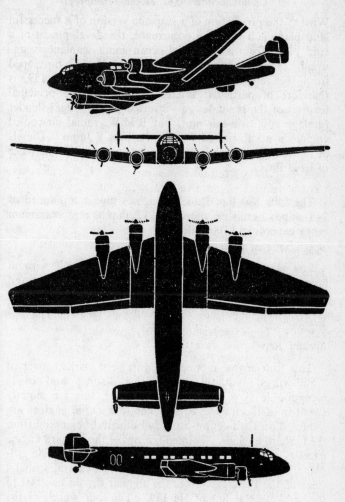

73

BLOHM & VOSS 142

Communication and Troop Transport

WHILST the production of a seaplane version of a successful land plane is a common occurrence, the development of a land plane from a successful ocean-going seaplane is unusual. The four-engine troop transport, Ha 142, developed from the long-range mail carrying seaplane Ha 139, is therefore of particular interest. It retains the principal features of the basic design—inverted " gull-wing," slender fuselage and twin-tail unit, but B.M.W. radial air-cooled engines are substituted for the Junkers " Jumo " Diesels of the Ha 139. A retractable undercarriage takes the place of fixed floats.

The four 880 h.p. B.M.W. engines give a top speed of 248 m.p.h., cruising speed of 217 m.p.h. and maximum range exceeding 2,700 miles.

Principal Structural Features

Low-wing monoplane, inverted " gull-wings " without taper, rounded tips ; four radial engines ; twin fins and rudders ; braced tailplane ; streamline fuselage of circular section. Undercarriage retracts into nacelles of inboard engines.

Special Recognition Points

This four-engine monoplane with very marked inverted " gull-wings," without taper, is a distinct and easily recognisable type. Wide rounded wing tips are slightly swept in at the trailing edge. The four radial engines are mounted on their centre-lines, full dihedral beginning from the inboard engines. Pointed fairings of the inboard engine nacelles project aft of the trailing edge. Rectangular tailplane, as in the Ha 139, is mounted on a central stub fin clear of the fuselage. Note the angular fins in contrast to the semi-circular fins of Ha 139. The four wheels of the undercarriage—two side-by-side pairs—are partially exposed when retracted.

BLOHM & VOSS Ha 142 (4–B.M.W. 132H)
Communication and Troop Transport
Span 96′ 9″   Length 64′ 0″   Height 15′ 6″

AIRCRAFT SILHOUETTES

SECTION II

MID-WING AND LOW MID-WING MONOPLANES

BREWSTER "BUFFALO"

Fighter

THIS new single-seat fighter which has earned the inevitable nickname of "flying barrel," is appropriately enough constructed by the Brewster Aeronautical Corporation of Long Island, N.Y.

Known by its makers as the "Brewster 339," it operates as a ship-borne fighter with the U.S. Navy under the designation F.2.A.–2. Orders for the same type were placed by the Belgian Government and diverted to the R.A.F.

In spite of the tubby appearance of the "Buffalo," it has a top speed exceeding 300 m.p.h. and is extremely manœuvrable. With special tankage, the maximum cruising range is 2,500 miles.

The power unit is either a single 850 h.p. Wright Cyclone radial air-cooled engine or a Pratt and Whitney Wasp of similar output.

A later version, the Brewster 439, fitted with a Wright Cyclone engine of 1,200 h.p., has a maximum speed around 330 m.p.h. Armament consists of six machine-guns, four of which are mounted in the wings.

Principal Structural Features

Low mid-wing monoplane, tapered wings with rounded tips, negligible dihedral; single radial engine; single fin and rudder. Short fuselage of circular section with glazed enclosed cockpit. Wheels retract into underside of fuselage.

Special Recognition Points

Wings have relatively short span and large chord; very slight taper on leading edge, full taper on trailing edge. Barrel-like appearance of nose and fuselage is very distinctive. Top of fuselage sweeps down to a finely streamlined tail. Fin is triangular, the rudder high and well rounded. Elliptical tailplane is mounted rather low on fuselage. The tail unit of the later version has been modified, being considerably wider at the base viewed from the side.

BREWSTER "BUFFALO"
Single–Seat Fighter
Span 35' 0"   Length 25' 6"

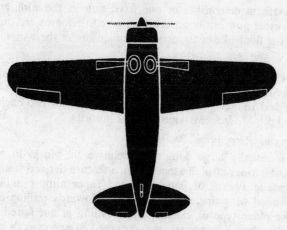

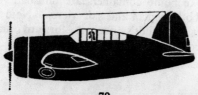

VICKERS "WELLESLEY"

DURING the two days from the 5th to the 7th November, 1938, Vickers "Wellesley" single engine monoplanes of the R.A.F. Long Range Development Unit, established a world's record for distance in a straight line by flying from Ismaila, Egypt, to Darwin, Australia, a non-stop flight of 7,162 miles. They covered the distance at an average speed of 149 m.p.h. The Wellesley's power unit is the Bristol "Pegasus XXII" radial air-cooled engine, developing 1,010 h.p. Apart from special tankage, the record-breaking machines were standard types. Top speed is 228 m.p.h. and maximum loaded range, with normal tankage exceeds 2,500 miles. The Vickers-Wallis geodetic system of construction, so successfully tested in the "Wellesley" design, was further developed in the "Wellesley's" successor, the twin-engine "Wellington."

Armament consists of one fixed gun in the wing and a movable gun in the observer's cockpit. Bombs are carried in the float-like containers suspended under the wings.

Principal Structural Features

Low mid-wing monoplane, tapered wings with slight dihedral and rounded tips ; single radial engine ; single fin and rudder ; fuselage of oval section with two enclosed cockpits. Undercarriage retracts inwards.

Special Recognition Points

Unusually large wing span relative to width, in other words, wings of high aspect ratio, a feature derived from the geodetic system of construction. Taper almost uniform, rounded wing tips, slightly swept in towards trailing·edge. The older type of exhaust ring cowling is not faired into the fuselage but appears semi-detached like an insect's head. The float-like bomb containers are unusual. Tail unit is distinctive both in plan and side views. Note the unusual arrangement of pilot's cockpit forward and separate observer's cockpit well aft.

WELLESLEY (Pegasus)
Bomber
Span 74' 7"   Length 39' 3"   Height 15' 4"

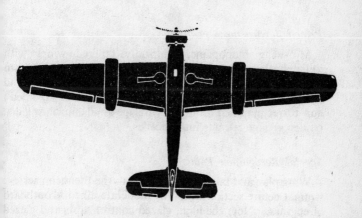

BRISTOL "BEAUFORT"

General Purpose

THE Bristol " Beaufort " (type 152), although having many points of resemblance to the famous Blenheim series, is specially designed as a torpedo-bomber-reconnaissance and general purpose plane. The power plant consists of two Bristol Taurus sleeve-valve air-cooled engines, each developing over 1,000 h.p. Actual performance figures are not available, but it is known to be appreciably faster than the Blenheims. The " Beaufort " design has been chosen for production in Australia, where it will probably be equipped with Australian-built Pratt & Whitney 750 h.p. Twin Wasp Junior engines.

Principal Structural Features

Mid-wing monoplane, uniformly tapered wings with rounded tips ; dihedral outboard of engines only. Two radial engines, three-quarters underslung ; single fin and rudder. Forward half of fuselage is deep and slab-sided ; gun-turret mounted on top of fuselage amidships facing aft. Undercarriage retracts into nacelles.

Special Recognition Points

Wing plan and tail unit are similar to the Blenheim series ; straight centre section with only moderate dihedral outboard of engines. Note the high, glazed control cabin and glazed bomb-aiming nose which projects forward of underslung engine nacelles. The deep forward section of fuselage ends abruptly amidships where rear turret is mounted. This " step-down " to the afterpart of normal Blenheim lines is distinctive.

82

BEAUFORT (2–Taurus)
General Purpose
Span 57' 10"   Length 44' 1½"   Height 14' 3"

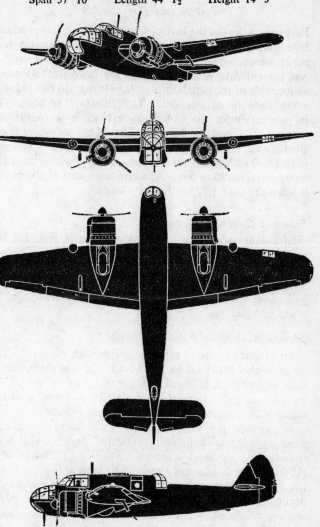

BLENHEIM 1

Fighter and Day Bomber

IN the early thirties the Bristol Aeroplane Company produced type 142, a twin-engined monoplane of exceptionally high performance. Subsequently christened " Britain First," it was presented to the Air Ministry by Lord Rothermere as an example of the capabilities of the British aircraft industry when suitably encouraged. The Bristol " Blenheim I " in production for the R.A.F. since 1936, is the militarised version of " Britain First." The Mk I or short-nosed Blenheim is largely used as a long-range fighter. Powered with two 840 h.p. Bristol Mercury radial engines, its maximum speed is 285 m.p.h. At a cruising speed of 200 m.p.h. it has a range of 1,125 miles fully loaded.

Principal Structural Features

Mid-wing monoplane, tapered wings with rounded tips and medium dihedral, increasing to full dihedral outboard of engines. Two radial engines mounted on their centre lines ; single fin and rudder ; streamline fuselage with rear gun-turret mounted on top, mid-way. Undercarriage retracts into nacelles.

Special Recognition Points

Short glazed nose is roughly in line with engines. This point is also observed in the Ju 88, but the projection of nose and engines is much more marked in the Ju 88. I equals nearly three-quarters of the wing chord, whilst in the case of Blenheim I it is less than half the chord.

Wings are gracefully tapered with fillet to fuselage. Leading edge of tailplane practically straight with well rounded elevator and large cut-away V—in contrast with rather angular tailplane of Ju 88. Side view of fuselage shows clean lines broken only by small gun-turret. Contrast this outline with high " conservatory " and low underslung engines of Ju 88. The " Blenheim " tail unit is smaller and of distinctive shape.

BLENHEIM I (2–Mercury)
Day Bomber
Span 56' 4"   Length 39' 9"   Height 9' 2"

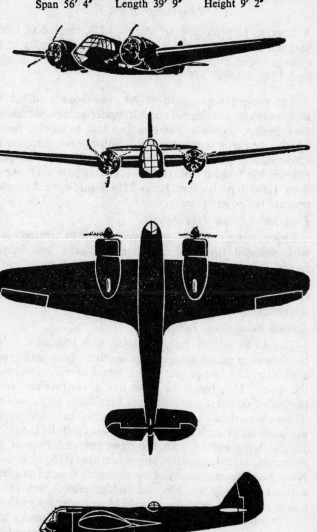

JUNKERS 88

Long-range Bomber

A JUNKERS 88 prototype, in March, 1939, created an international record, carrying a two-ton load 620 miles at an average speed of 321 m.p.h. In July it carried a similar load 1240 miles at 311 m.p.h.

The present version, Ju 88–A1, has been modified by such additions as enlarged cockpit, under-gun emplacement, dive brakes, external bomb-racks, and a special device which, synchronised with the bomb-release mechanism, automatically pulls out of a diving attack when the pilot releases his bombs. Maximum speed is now 317 m.p.h. Two 1,200 h.p. Junkers Jumo 211A liquid-cooled engines provide the power plant.

Principal Structural Features

Low mid-wing monoplane, unsymmetrically tapered wings with rounded tips and moderate dihedral; two liquid cooled in-line engines with radiator in the form of *radial cowlings*. Single fin and rudder; streamline fuselage with short glazed nose and large "conservatory" forward undercarriage retracts into nacelles.

Special Recognition Points

The Ju 88 is frequently confused with Blenheim I, but the following points are quite distinctive: oversize engines are underslung and project well forward of wing, level with the nose. They break the lower line of the fuselage whilst the high "conservatory" forward breaks the upper outline. These characteristics give the Ju 88 a nose-heavy appearance not observed in the Blenheim. Compare carefully the rather angular wing outline with the more graceful lines of the Blenheim, which has a curved streamline fillet at the wing roots. Note the similar angularity of the uniformly tapered tailplane without cut-away V. Fin and rudder project well aft of tailplane. In the head-on view the large underslung engines are characteristic. The four external bomb-racks and under-gun emplacement, off centre, may be observed.

JUNKERS Ju. 88 A-1. (Jumo 211A)
Long–Range Bomber
Span 59′ 0″   Length 46′ 6″   Height 15′ 0″

BLENHEIM MK. IV

Medium Bomber

THE Blenheim IV, or long-nosed version, is developed from
and closely resembles Mk. I. It is easily distinguished
from the earlier design—as also from Ju 88—by the nose,
which, nearly three feet longer, projects well forward of
the engines. With two Bristol Mercury radial air-cooled
engines developing 930 h.p., Mk. IV has a maximum speed
of 295 m.p.h. fully loaded, and a range of 2,000 miles.

Mk. IV *modified* (Mk. IV F) may be distinguished by a
gun position projecting below the nose.

The Bristol Bolingbroke is a Canadian-built version of
Blenheim IV, now in service with the Royal Canadian Air
Force. Pratt & Whitney Twin Wasp Junior engines of
750 h.p. are fitted as alternatives to Bristol Mercury engines.
Additional versions of the Bolingbroke may be fitted with
skis or floats.

Principal Structural Features

Mid-wing monoplane, tapered wings with rounded tips
and medium dihedral, increasing to full dihedral outboard
of engines. Two radial engines mounted on their centre
lines ; single fin and rudder ; streamline fuselage with rear
gun-turret mounted on top midway. Undercarriage retracts
into nacelles.

Special Recognition Points

Nose with glazed bomb-aiming panels above and below
projects well forward of engines. Wings are gracefully
tapered with fillet to fuselage. Leading edge of tailplane
practically straight with well-rounded elevator and large
cut-away V—in contrast with rather angular tailplane of
Ju 88. Side view of fuselage shows clean lines broken
only by small gun-turret. Contrast this outline with high
" conservatory " and low underslung engines of Ju 88.
The " Blenheim " tail unit is smaller and of distinctive
shape.

BLENHEIM IV (2–Mercury)
Medium Bomber
Span 56′ 4″   Length 42′ 7″   Height 9′ 2″

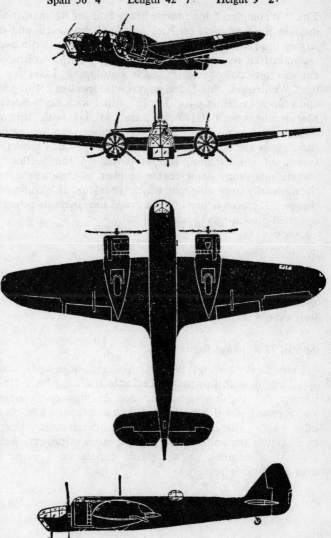

VICKERS " WELLINGTON "

THE " Wellington " long-range heavy bomber distinguished itself in the first raids on Kiel and Wilhelmshaven and is largely used for bombing distant targets such as Berlin and the industrial regions of Northern Italy. With two Bristol Pegasus air-cooled engines, each developing 1,000 h.p., the " Wellington " Mk IA has a maximum speed of 250 m.p.h. and cruises at 232 m.p.h. Mk II is fitted with Rolls-Royce Merlin engines of 1,145 h.p., and Mk III with Bristol " Hercules " engines of 1,375 h.p. Performance figures of these types are not available. The Vickers-Wallis geodetic system of construction, first employed in the Wellesley special long-range single-engine bomber, is responsible for the unusually large wing span which is a feature of Wellington design. German fighters have learned to respect its power-operated gun-turrets in nose and tail.

Principal Structural Features

Mid-wing monoplane, fully tapered wings with moderate dihedral. Two radial, alternatively two in-line engines, mounted on their centre lines. Large single fin and rudder. Retractable undercarriage.

Special Recognition Points

Fully tapered wings have particularly large span and small chord, with tips rounded off into trailing edge. Unusually tall angular fin and rudder set high on fuselage and forward of tail turret. Tailplane has taper on leading edge only. Turret projects well behind tail unit. Deep oval section streamline fuselage ; glazed nose projects well forward of engines. Small glazed cupola or " pimple " over navigator's seat.

WELLINGTON (2–Pegasus)
Bomber
Span 86′ 2″   Length 61′ 0″   Height 22′ 2″

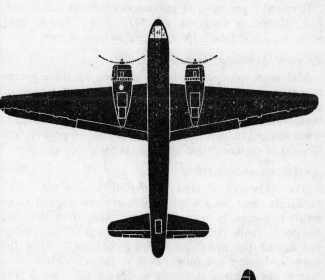

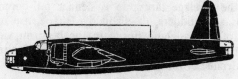

HANDLEY PAGE "HAMPDEN" AND "HEREFORD"

Medium Bombers

EMPLOYED chiefly for medium-range work, the " Hampden," successor to the Handley Page " Harrow," has played a notable part in the daily R.A.F. raids on oil storage plants, communications and the heavy industries of the Ruhr. Pilot and crew are accommodated forward, the after part of the fuselage being little more than a boom carrying the tail unit. In addition to the pilot's fixed gun, there are three movable gun positions ; in the nose, in the top of the fuselage amidships and immediately beneath the trailing edge. The " Hampden," fitted with two 1,000 h.p. Bristol Pegasus XVIII air-cooled radial engines, has a top speed of 265 m.p.h. and cruises at 217 m.p.h. The Handley-Page " Hereford," produced at the works of Short & Harland, Ltd., Belfast, is similar to the "Hampden," but is fitted with two 1,000 h.p. Napier Dagger in-line engines.

Principal Structural Features

Mid-wing monoplane ; wings tapering on trailing edge to narrow square-cut tips ; dihedral on outer section of wings only. " *Hampden*," two radial engines ; " *Hereford*," two in-line engines ; engines mounted on their centre lines. Twin fins and rudders ; glazed nose of fuselage projects well forward of engines ; undercarriage retracts into nacelles.

Special Recognition Points

The " Hampden " (and " Hereford ") wing plan, with negligible taper on leading edge and very marked taper on trailing edge, is most distinctive. Seen from the side, the deep narrow slab-sided forward section of the fuselage has earned the nickname " Flying Suitcase." Note the upper and lower gun-turrets both facing aft. From these turrets the fuselage tapers to a slender tail-boom. The twin fins and rudders, of distinctive shape, are mounted inboard of the tailplane tips. In the head-on view they can be seen slightly inboard of the centre lines of the engines. The underside of the retracted wheels is visible.

HAMPDEN (2–Pegasus)
Bomber
Span 69′ 4″   Length 53′ 7″   Height 14′ 9″

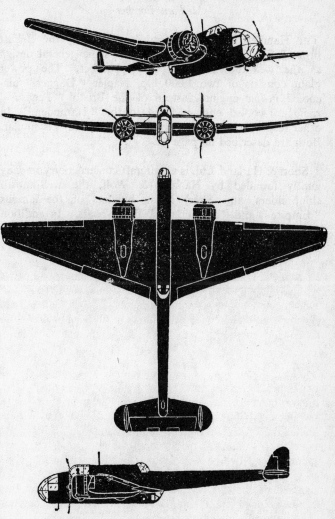

HANDLEY PAGE "HEREFORD"

Medium Bomber

THE Handley Page "Hereford" is built by the Belfast firm of Short & Harland Ltd. to the same general design as the well-known "Hampden" bomber. The power plant consists of two 1,000 h.p. Napier "Dagger" air-cooled *in-line* engines instead of the Bristol "Pegasus" *radial* air-cooled engines fitted to the "Hampden." In other respects the appearance of the two versions is similar. Both are described on page 92.

Short & Harland Ltd. is an aircraft construction company jointly founded by Harland & Wolf, the well-known shipbuilders, and Short Bros., builders of the famous "Empire" and "Sunderland" flying-boats. In addition to "Hereford" bombers the company also builds the Bristol "Bombay" troop transport.

HEREFORD (2–Dagger)
Bomber
Span 69' 4" Length 53' 7" Height 14' 9"

LOCKHEED HUDSON

FIRST of the American machines to be delivered in quantity to the R.A.F. and the Royal Australian Air Force, the " Hudson " is the military version of the well-known Lockheed 14 trans-continental air liner, big brother of the Lockheed " Electra " which carried Mr. Chamberlain and his umbrella to the ill-starred conference with Hitler.

Powered with two Wright Cyclone engines of 1,100 h.p., its maximum speed is 246 m.p.h. At the economical cruising speed of 170 m.p.h. it has a range of 1,700 miles. " Hudsons " have been extensively used as reconnaissance bombers by the Coastal Command. Their power-operated gun-turret near the tail enables them to deal satisfactorily with enemy interception.

Principal Structural Features

Low mid-wing monoplane ; wings fully tapered to semi-pointed tips, with full dihedral ; two radial engines ; twin fins and rudders ; deep roomy double-deck streamline fuselage with glazed bomb-aiming nose ; large domed turret on top of fuselage, well aft. Retractable undercarriage.

Special Recognition Points

Plan view : Pronounced taper of wings. Note guides for Fowler flaps projecting from trailing edge between fuselage and ailerons. Nose projects well forward of engines. Tailplane chiefly tapered on leading edge has rounded tips and unusually large span.

Side view : Engine nacelles two-thirds underslung, show part of retracted wheels. Large pear-shaped fin and rudder is mounted just in-board of tailplane tips ; outline of fuselage from deep low nose to shallow high tail is characteristic.

Head-on view : Full dihedral ; underslung engines ; note the position of fins and rudders and domed turret on top of deep oval-section fuselage.

HUDSON (2–Wright Cyclone)
Reconnaissance Bomber
Span 65′ 6″   Length 44′ 4″   Height 11′ 10½″

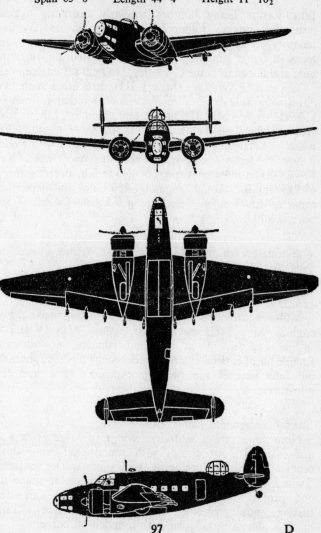

ARMSTRONG-WHITWORTH "WHITLEY"

LONG-RANGE heavy bomber regularly operating against industrial targets hundreds of miles inside German territory, or as far afield as northern Italy, non-stop from bases in Great Britain. The power-operated gun-turret in nose and tail enables the "Whitley" to fight off interceptors. The earlier Whitleys (Mks I–III), are fitted with two Armstrong-Siddeley "Tiger" air-cooled radial engines of 850–918 h.p. Mk III has a top speed of 215 m.p.h., cruising speed of 177 m.p.h. and range of about 1,300 miles. Later types (Mks IV and V) are fitted with Rolls-Royce "Merlin" engines, developing over 1,000 h.p. Mk IV has a maximum speed of 245 m.p.h., cruising speed of 215 m.p.h., normal range of 1,250 miles and maximum range of 1,800 miles. Performance figures for Mk V are not available.

Silhouettes of the Merlin-engined Whitleys are on page 101.

Principal Structural Features

Mid-wing monoplane, tapered wings of large span; two engines, Mks I–III have radial engines, Mks IV and V in-line engines. Twin fins and rudders, fins braced. Engine nacelles three-quarters under-slung; wheels, retracting into nacelles, are partially exposed. Nose and tail gun-turret.

Special Recognition Points

Nose-down flying attitude. Wings of large span and unusual width, or chord, with rounded-off wing tips; moderate dihedral beginning well outboard of engines. Twin fins and rudders of characteristic angular shape do not project below tailplane. Long narrow slab-sided fuselage, nose projecting well forward of engines. Tailplane is almost rectangular with rounded-off corners.

WHITLEY (2–Tiger) Mk I
Bomber
Span 84′ 0″   Length 69′ 3″   Height 15′ 0″

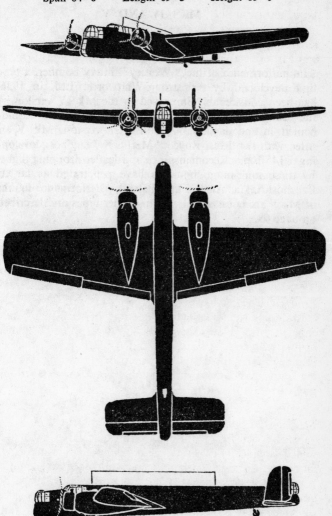

ARMSTRONG-WHITWORTH " WHITLEY "

MKS IV AND V

Long-range Heavy Bombers

THE performance of the " Whitley " heavy bomber, a type
first developed by Armstrong-Whitworth, Ltd. in 1936,
has been considerably improved in the Mk IV version by
the fitting of 1,030 h.p. Rolls-Royce " Merlin IV " liquid-
cooled in-line engines. A still later version, Mk V, is
fitted with two Rolls-Royce " Merlin X " engines, developing 1,145 h.p. Reconnaissance and leaflet-dropping flights
by these long-range bombers have penetrated as far as
Czechoslovakia, Austria and Poland. Performance figures
of Mk V are not available. The earlier types are described
on page 98.

WHITLEY IV and V (2–Merlin)
Bomber
Span 84′ 0″   Length 70′ 6″   Height 15′ 0″

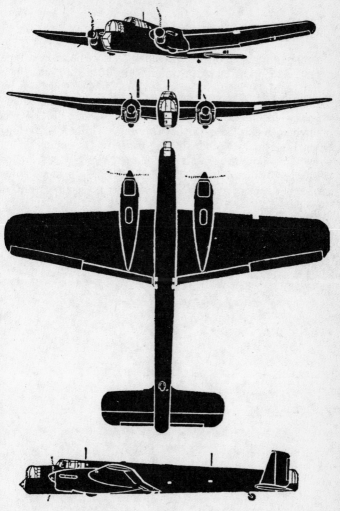

AIRCRAFT SILHOUETTES

SECTION III

HIGH-WING MONOPLANES

WESTLAND "LYSANDER"

Army Co-operation

DESIGNED throughout for co-operation with an army in the field, this two-seater monoplane has many interesting features. It excels in ability to operate from small improvised flying fields, its take-off run to clear a fifty-foot obstacle being only 245 yards. With a useful maximum speed of 230 m.p.h., it can nevertheless fly fully loaded as slowly as 55 m.p.h. These figures refer to Mark II, fitted with a 905 h.p. Bristol Perseus sleeve-valve air-cooled radial engine. Mark I is fitted with the Bristol Mercury radial engine of 890 h.p., which gives approximately the same performance.

In addition to the observer's gun, a machine-gun is fixed in each of the wheel " spats " firing forward, clear of the airscrew. Detachable stub-wings, designed as carriers for light bombs or special equipment, can be fitted above the wheel " spats." A retractable hook enables the " Lysander " to collect messages.

Principal Structural Features.

High-wing monoplane, braced, wings of distinctive plan with half-rounded tips ; no dihedral. Single radial engine ; single fin and rudder ; deep fuselage with large two-seat glazed cockpit. Fixed undercarriage with large wheel-spats.

Special Recognition Points

Easily recognisable " dragonfly " wings braced by V-struts ; centre section of leading edge tapers *inboard* to give better observation. Trailing edges are fully tapered on the outboard section only. Glazed roof of large cockpit separates the wing roots. Large angular fin and rudder, with rounded top, high on fuselage ; tailplane of long chord and rounded tips, is placed low on fuselage, right aft. Spatted undercarriage is particularly distinctive when stub wings are fitted.

LYSANDER (Mercury)
Army Co-operation
Span 50′ 0″   Length 30′ 0″   Height 14′ 0″

HENSCHEL 126

Army Co-operation

THE Henschel 126 two-seat monoplane has something of the insect-like appearance of the R.A.F. " Lysander." It fulfils similar roles—photography, artillery spotting, communications and general reconnaissance. Powered with a B.M.W. radial air-cooled engine, developing 870 h.p., it has a maximum speed of 229 m.p.h. Armament consists of one fixed gun, firing through the airscrew disc, and one observer's gun, in contrast with the three guns of the " Lysander." Comparison of the two machines also suggests that the field of vision from the " Henschel " cockpit is inferior to that from the " Lysander " " conservatory."

Principal Structural Features

High wing monoplane, braced, of parasol type ; wings swept back to rounded tips ; trailing edge swept *forward* towards the wing roots ; no dihedral. Single radial engine ; single fin and rudder ; streamline fuselage of oval section ; fixed undercarriage, spatted wheels.

Special Recognition Points

In spite of a superficial resemblance to the " Lysander," these points are distinctive : Leading edge of " Henschel " wings projects forward of pilot's seat forming a wide V. " Lysander's " leading edge is *cut away* to clear pilot's line of vision. " Henschel " wings have deep V-shape cut-away in the trailing edge over the observer's seat. The wings are not separated by glazed cabin roof as in " Lysander." Note the additional wing struts near centre section. Tail unit is smaller, tailplane of large span and small chord is carried *high* and is braced. Radial engine has fluted cowling. Wheel " spats " are noticeably smaller than " Lysander's."

HENSCHEL 126
Army Co-operation
Span 47' 7"   Length 35' 7"   Height 12' 4"

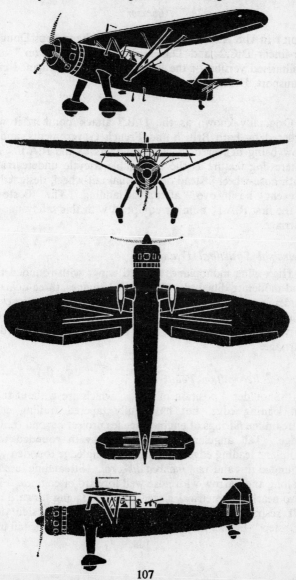

DOUGLAS "BOSTON"

Bomber

BUILT in U.S.A. by the constructors of the famous Douglas air-liners D.C.2 and D.C.3, the R.A.F. "Boston" is a militarised version of the latest Douglas twin-engined civil transport, D.C.5.

Originally known as the D.B.7 attack bomber, it was ordered by both British and French Governments, and is now being delivered in large numbers to the R.A.F. An interesting feature is the retractable tricycle undercarriage with nose-wheel instead of the usual tail-wheel, designed to prevent " nosing over " after a bad landing. The " Boston " is the first R.A.F. bomber equipped with this safety under-carriage.

Principal Structural Features

High-wing monoplane, tapered wings with rounded tips and moderate dihedral. Two radial engines, three-quarters underslung ; single tall fin and rudder ; streamline fuselage with glazed panels in nose, glazed roof to control cabin forward and gun position aft. Retractable tricycle under-carriage.

Special Recognition Points

" Shoulder " position of wings, which are without taper on leading edge, but have fully tapered trailing edge. Streamline fairings of engine nacelles project beyond trailing edge. Tall angular fin and rudder with rounded top ; tailplane leading edge is tapered, trailing edge rounded with rounded tips and *very marked dihedral*. Streamline fuselage is long and narrow with nose well forward of engines. The two nearly symmetrical glazed sections, facing forward and aft respectively, give a distinctive outline. In side view, a " step " breaks the line of the fuselage below the tail unit.

BOSTON (2–Cyclone)
Bomber
Span 61' 4"   Length 47' 0"   Height 16' 0"

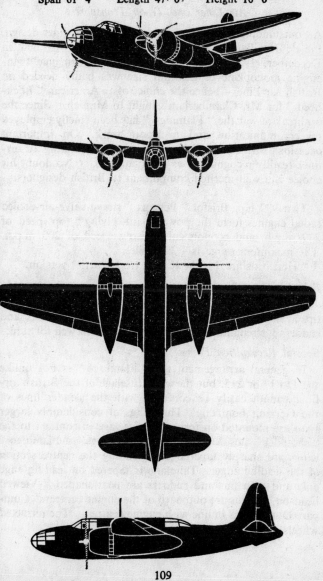

DE HAVILLAND "FLAMINGO"

Air Liner and Troop Transport

AN outstanding example of modern British air-liner design, the de Havilland "Flamingo" or D.H. 95, first flew in December, 1938. This type of high performance twin-engine monoplane of medium size was badly needed on British Air Lines—hence the choice of an American "Lockheed" for Mr. Chamberlain's flight to Munich. Since the outbreak of war the "Flamingo" has been chiefly employed on communication and transport work. On important occasions Mr. Churchill has been pictured entering an air-liner readily recognisable as a "Flamingo." No doubt his choice is a well-merited compliment to British designers.

Two 930 h.p. Bristol "Perseus" sleeve-valve air-cooled radial engines form the power plant, giving a top speed of 239 m.p.h. and economical cruising speed of 200 m.p.h. The maximum range is 1,300 miles.

"Hertfordshire" is the R.A.F. troop-carrier version.

Principal Structural Features

High-wing monoplane, wings tapering to semi-pointed tips ; no dihedral. Two radial engines ; twin fins and rudders ; streamline fuselage ; control cabin well forward.

Special Recognition Points

In general arrangement the "Flamingo" is not unlike the Do 17 or 215, but the large fuselage of the British air-liner cannot easily be confused with the slender lines of the German bombers. The wings of considerably larger span are mounted on top of the fuselage in contrast to the "shoulder" position of the Dornier wings. "Flamingo" wings are sharply tapered except along the centre section of the leading edge. Tailplane is tapered on leading edge only and twin fins and rudders are pear-shaped. Viewed head-on, the fins are outboard of the engine centres. Compare Dornier fins in line with engine centres. The retracted wheels are partially exposed.

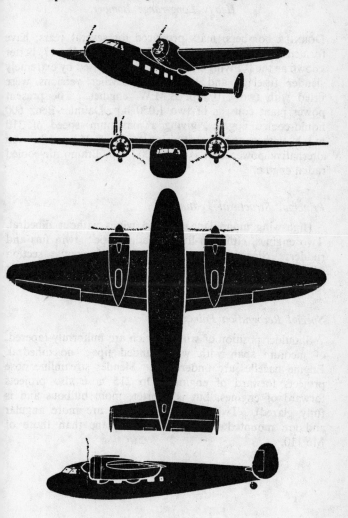

DORNIER 17

Heavy Long-range Bomber

DORNIER bombers, mass produced for several years, have formed the backbone of the Luftwaffe. The Do 17, better known as the " Flying Pencil," is characterised by extremely slender fuselage and long nose. Earlier versions were fitted with two 770 h.p. B.M.W. engines. The present power plant consists of two 1,050 h.p. Daimler-Benz 600 liquid-cooled engines, giving a maximum speed of 310 m.p.h. with economical cruising speed of 242 m.p.h. An alternative power unit is the 1,000 h.p. Bramo air-cooled radial engine.

Principal Structural Features

High-wing monoplane, tapered wings without dihedral. Two engines, either in-line or radial type ; twin fins and rudders. Slender streamline fuselage of circular section with nose projecting forward of engines. Wheels retract into engine nacelles ; tail wheel also retracts.

Special Recognition Points

Shoulder position of wings, which are uniformly tapered, of medium span with well-rounded tips ; no dihedral. Engine nacelles are underslung. Slender streamline nose projects forward of engines (Do 215 nose also projects forward of engines, but is shorter, more bulbous and is fully glazed). Twin fins and rudders are more angular and are mounted higher on the tailplane than those of Me 110.

DORNIER 17 (D.B. Engines)
Bomber
Span 59' 0"   Length 55' 4"   Height 15' 0"

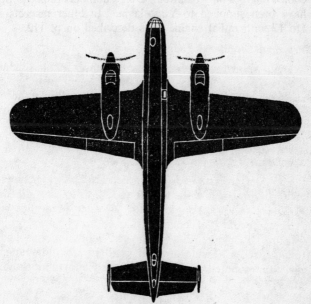

DORNIER 17

Heavy Bomber

THE appearance of the " Flying Pencil " or Do 17 is considerably changed by the fitting of large *radial* engines such as the 1,000 h.p. " Bramo " air-cooled radial engines depicted in the silhouettes facing this page. Compare these silhouettes with those on p. 113, which show Do 17 fitted with liquid-cooled *in-line* engines.

Alternatively, two 1,000 h.p. Gnome-Rhone radial air-cooled engines may be fitted. Do 17 bombers thus equipped have been supplied to Yugoslavia. In other respects the Do 17 with radial engine is as described on p. 112.

DORNIER 17 (Bramo 323 Engines)
Bomber
Span 59′ 0″   Length 55′ 4″   Height 15′ 0″

DORNIER 215

Long-range Heavy Bomber

DEVELOPED from the Do 17 design, the Do 215 closely resembles the earlier type, the modifications chiefly affecting the fuselage forward of the wings. The Do 215 nose is shorter and is completely covered with glazed panels. The deep cockpit forward of the wings accommodates a crew of four and is enclosed by a domed glazed top or "conservatory." The power plant is usually two 1,150 h.p. Daimler-Benz 601A liquid-cooled engines, with alternative installations as for Do 17. The performance is similar, maximum speed being 312 m.p.h. At cruising speed of 264 m.p.h. the range is just under 1,000 miles.

Principal Structural Features

High-wing monoplane, tapered wings without dihedral. Two engines, either in-line or radial type; twin fins and rudders. Slender streamline fuselage of circular section with deep forward section and large glazed "conservatory." Wheels retract into engine nacelles; tail wheel also retracts.

Special Recognition Points

Shoulder position of wings, which are uniformly tapered of medium span with well-rounded tips; no dihedral. Engine nacelles underslung; fully glazed nose project forward of engines, but is much shorter than that of Do 17. "Conservatory" roof extends almost to the nose. Tail unit is the same as Do 17.

DORNIER 215
Bomber
Span 59' 0"   Length 53' 6"   Height 15' 9"

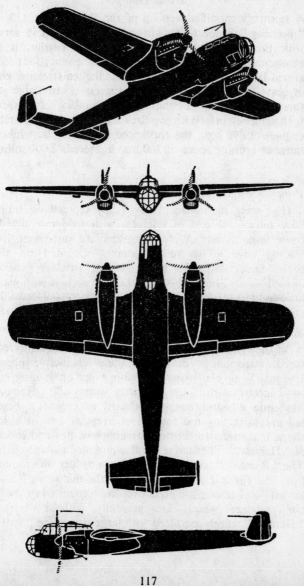

BRISTOL "BOMBAY"

Troop Transport

A SLIGHTLY modified version of the Bristol type 130, the
" Bombay " is the only twin-tail Bristol design in service
with the R.A.F. Employed as a troop carrier, it has
accommodation for a crew of three and twenty-four fully
armed troops. Alternatively it can take ten stretcher cases
or heavy loads of equipment and spares. Formidable gun
turrets in nose and tail enable the " Bombay " to dispense
with fighter escort. With two Bristol Pegasus air-cooled radial
engines of 890 h.p., the top speed is 192 m.p.h., whilst its
range at cruising speed of 160 m.p.h. exceeds 2,000 miles.

Principal Structural Features

High-wing monoplane, wings fully tapered on trailing
edge only, outboard of engines, with moderate dihedral
from same point. Wide wing-tips are out-swept from
leading edge. Two radial engines mounted on their
centre lines ; twin fins and rudders ; fuselage generally
of oval section, but slab-sided in centre section with glazed
nose and tail-turrets. Tapered nose projects well forward of
engines ; fixed undercarriage wheels usually without " spats."

Special Recognition Points

As the " Bombay " and " Harrow " are frequently confused, attention is drawn to these distinctive points.
Unusual wing plan with negligible taper on leading edge
in contrast with fully tapered wings of " Harrow."
Moderate dihedral begins outboard of engines ; braced
tail unit with fins and rudders of irregular oval or kidney
shape in contrast to the angular unbraced fins and rudders
of " Harrow." The latter are also mounted closer together.
The " Bombay " tailplane has little or no taper with rounded
tips. Its fuselage appears to sag in the middle as if overloaded—a characteristic aspect readily recognised in the air.
Undercarriage wheels are generally without " spats."
" Harrow " wheels are fitted with large streamline " spats."

118

BOMBAY I (2 Pegasus)
Transport
Span 95′ 9″   Length 69′ 2″   Height 19′ 11″

HANDLEY PAGE "HARROW"

Bomber-Transport

THE Handley Page "Harrow" came into regular service as a heavy bomber of the R.A.F. in 1936. Like the Bristol "Bombay," for which it is frequently mistaken, it is now chiefly used as a troop carrier and for general transport work. Its armament is similar, consisting of gun-turret in nose and tail, with a third gun position aft of the wings. The earlier type equipped with two Bristol Pegasus X air-cooled radial engines, has a top speed of 190 m.p.h. and cruising speed of 154 m.p.h. The later, or Mk. II Harrow, fitted with Pegasus XX engines, is faster by about ten m.p.h. Its maximum range is close on 2,000 miles.

Principal Structural Features

High-wing monoplane, fully tapered wings with moderate dihedral. Two radial engines mounted on their centre lines ; twin fins and rudders ; slab-sided fuselage with nose and tail turrets, nose projecting well forward of engines. Fixed spatted undercarriage.

Special Recognition Points

Note, in contrast with the "Bombay," the fully tapered wings with square-cut tips, and the generally more angular appearance of the "Harrow." The angular fins and rudders with rounded tips are particularly distinctive. These are not braced and are set closer together than those of the "Bombay." Note the large streamlined wheel "spats" in contrast with the usually unspatted wheels of the "Bombay." The centre section of the fuselage has not the overloaded sagging appearance which characterises the "Bombay."

HARROW (2 Pegasus)
Bomber—Transport
Span 88′ 5″   Length 82′ 1″   Height 20′ 2″

AIRCRAFT SILHOUETTES

SECTION IV

FLOAT-SEAPLANES AND FLYING BOATS

HEINKEL 115

Torpedo Bomber Reconnaissance

SHORTLY before the war this type of high performance float-seaplane established several international records, including a flight of 1,242 miles at an average speed of 204 m.p.h. with load of nearly two tons. This performance is of special interest in view of the Heinkel's present activities, which include torpedo carrying and mine laying. The He 115 has also been reported in action as a troop carrier, particularly round the Dutch and Norwegian coasts.

The design is developed from and broadly resembles that of the long-range bomber Heinkel 111K. The power plant, consisting of two 880 h.p. B.M.W. radial air-cooled engines, gives a maximum speed of 220 m.p.h., cruising speed of 183 m.p.h. and range of 1,300 miles.

Principal Structural Features

Mid-wing monoplane, float seaplane. Tapered wings with moderate dihedral and rounded tips ; two radial engines mounted near their centre lines ; single fin and rudder ; long slender fuselage of oval section ; fixed twin floats.

Special Recognition Points

Taper of wings is more marked on leading edge, outboard of engines. Wing is not unlike that of He 111 Mk. V without the " bite " out of the trailing edge. Slender streamline fuselage resembles the long-nose version of He 111K, but fin is very angular with square-cut top and rectangular rudder. Braced tailplane high on fuselage, shows a similar angularity, but has rounded tips. Glazed nose of Mk. III projects forward of floats. Earlier types have shorter nose. Large " conservatory." Notice the slender " N " struts of the float undercarriage in contrast to the wide tubular undercarriage legs of the Blohm & Voss float-planes.

HEINKEL 115
Torpedo Bomber Reconnaissance
Span 73' 0"   Length 56' 8"

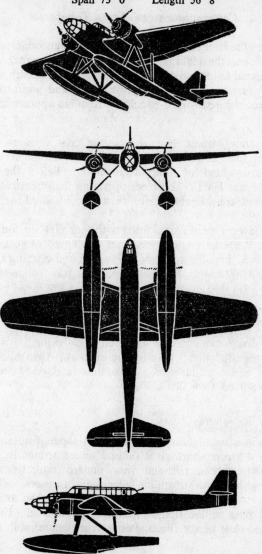

BLOHM & VOSS Ha 139

Communication and Troop Transport

BUILT by the Hamburg subsidiary of the well-known German shipbuilders, the Ha 139, four-engine float seaplane, is no less original in design than the 138. The unusually long, slender fuselage, inverted " gull-wings " and short squat legs gives this seaplane a peculiarly reptilian appearance.

Like the Dornier flying boats, the civil versions were built for the Lufthansa North and South Atlantic services, and are designed for catapult launching. Before the outbreak of war Ha 139 seaplanes operating these services had completed considerably more than one hundred Atlantic crossings.

The latest type, 139B, is fitted with four 600 h.p. Junkers " Jumo " Diesel engines, giving a top speed of just over 200 m.p.h., cruising speed of 167 m.p.h. and cruising range of over 3,000 miles. A recent development is the landplane version, Ha 142.

Principal Structural Features

Low-wing monoplane. Inverted " gull-wing," without taper, rounded tips ; four in-line engines ; twin fins and rudders on braced tailplane ; streamline fuselage of circular section ; fixed twin floats.

Special Recognition Points

The inverted " gull-wings " without taper, four in-line engines and the short squat tubular undercarriage legs are most characteristic. In side view, undercarriage legs have great width, due to streamline fairings or " trousers." Twin fins and rudders of distinctive shape are attached at their centres near to the tips of the braced tailplane. This is mounted clear of the fuselage on a short central stub fin.

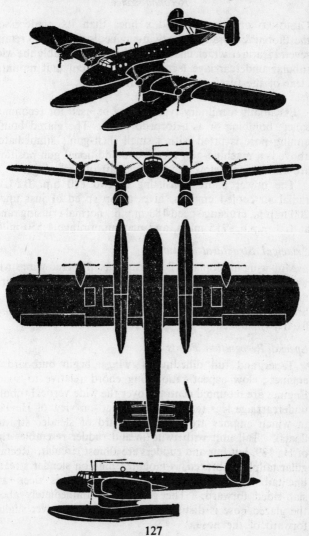

BLOHM & VOSS 140

Reconnaissance

DESIGNED on more orthodox lines than its predecessor, the Blohm & Voss Ha 140 twin-engine float seaplane retains several features which characterised Ha 139, notably the wide tubular undercarriage legs and the twin tail unit mounted clear of the fuselage on a central stub fin.

Essentially a military type, it may be used for reconnaissance, bombing or as a torpedo plane. The glazed bomb-aiming nose is fitted with a small shell-gun; immediately above is a machine-gun turret, and additional gun positions are above and below the fuselage, aft of the wings.

The power plant, consisting of two 880 h.p. B.M.W. radial air-cooled engines, gives a top speed of just under 200 m.p.h., cruising speed 183 m.p.h., normal cruising range at 160 m.p.h., 715 miles, and maximum range 1,550 miles.

Principal Structural Features

Mid-wing monoplane, float seaplane. Tapered wings with wide rounded tips and dihedral; twin radial engines mounted on their centre lines. Twin fins and rudders; braced tailplane; streamline fuselage with glazed nose; fixed twin floats.

Special Recognition Points

Taper and full dihedral of wings begin outboard of engines; low aspect ratio (long chord relative to span). Engines are mounted centrally over the wide vertical tubular undercarriage legs (compare with head-on view of He 115, in which engines are slightly inboard of slender strutted floats). Tail unit with twin fin and rudder resembles that of Ha 139, but fins and rudders are almost circular. Rectangular tailplane, braced, is mounted high on slender streamline tail. Fuselage of roughly oval section is deep and slab-sided forward. The gun cupola immediately above the glazed nose is distinctive. Fixed floats project slightly forward of the nose.

BLOHM & VOSS Ha 140
Reconnaissance
Span 69' 0"   Length 57' 9"

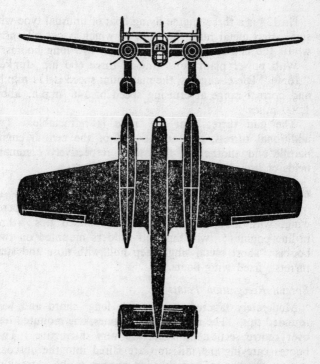

BLOHM & VOSS Ha 138

Reconnaissance Flying Boat

BLOHM & VOSS, well-known German shipbuilders, entered the aircraft industry several years ago, and through their subsidiary company, the Hamburger Flugzeugbau, are responsible for at least four interesting types now in service with the Luftwaffe. These are the Ha 138, 139, 140 and 142, the abbreviation " Ha " indicating the constructing company.

Ha 138 is a three-engine flying boat of unusual type with single-step metal hull, the stern of which is cut off short, whilst the tail unit is carried high on two long booms.

With power plant consisting of three 600 h.p. Junkers " Jumo " Diesel engines, the maximum speed is 171 m.p.h., and normal range at cruising speed of 146 m.p.h. about 1,500 miles.

The gun turret near the nose is retractable. Two additional turrets, one at the end of the central engine nacelle and another in the stern, respectively command fields of fire above and below the tail boom.

Principal Structural Features

Flying boat, high-wing monoplane. Very slightly tapered wings with moderate dihedral and rounded tips ; three in-line engines ; twin fins and rudders mounted on twin booms ; short metal single-step hull with nose and stern turrets ; fixed wing-floats.

Special Recognition Points

Moderately tapered wings with long chord and wide rounded tips. The three in-line engines, one mounted high over centre section of wing, are very distinctive. Twin booms carrying the tail unit are faired into the outboard engine nacelles, of which they appear to be extensions. Twin fins and rudders are carried high and well aft of the stern, with rectangular tailplane mounted between booms. Braced fixed floats are near the wing tips.

BLOHM & VOSS Ha 138
Reconnaissance
Span 88' 7"   Length 65' 4"   Hull 49' 6"

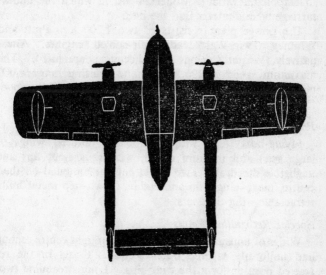

CONSOLIDATED PBY 5 (28-5)
(Catalina)
Reconnaissance

In 1939 a Consolidated PBY flying-boat, purchased for R.A.F. tests, was flown 5,700 miles from California to the Experimental Station at Felixstowe, with only one stop for refueling at Botwood, Newfoundland, thus completing the first delivery flight across the Atlantic. Large numbers have now been ordered for the R.A.F.

Built by the Consolidated Aircraft Corporation of San Diego, more than 250 of the PBY series of flying-boats have been supplied to the U.S. Navy. The civil version is well known as Consolidated Model 28. There is also an amphibian variant, Model 28–5A, in which the undercarriage wheels retract into the hull.

The power plant consists of two 1,200 h.p. Pratt and Whitney Twin-Wasp radial air-cooled engines. Alternatively, Wright Cyclone radial engines are fitted. The maximum speed is 206 m.p.h. and cruising range 4,000 miles. Performance on one engine is exceptionally good. Details of armament are not yet released.

Principal Structural Features

Flying-boat, high wing monoplane. Braced wings of large span and medium chord, with square-cut tips and negligible dihedral. Two radial engines mounted on their centre lines ; single fin and rudder ; two-step metal hull ; retractable wing-tip floats.

Special Recognition Points

Wings of unusually large span with straight centre section and uniformly tapered outer section. Floats in the retracted position form the wing-tips. Long streamline two-step hull terminates in a slender " fish-tail," the fin, rudder and high tailplane forming a most characteristic tail unit. The absence of fixed wing-floats distinguishes the PBY series from British flying-boats.

CONSOLIDATED PBY5
Reconnaissance Bomber. Crew 6
Span 104′ 0″   Length 62′ 6″   Height 18′ 6″

DORNIER 18
Reconnaissance (or Bomber) Flying Boat

LESS widely known than its immediate predecessor Do 17, or " Flying Pencil," the Do 18 twin-engine flying boat has an excellent record in civil aviation. Built by the firm which produced the world's largest flying boat, the twelve-engined giant Do X, the Do 18 was developed from the successful Dornier " Wal " flying boats, which first opera ted a regular South Atlantic mail service. Like the " Wal," the Do 18 flying boats are designed for catapult launching. In 1936 a Do 18 made the first crossing of the North Atlantic by regular passenger flying boat. After refuelling at the Azores it was catapult-launched from the mother ship *Schwabenland*, continuing non-stop to New York. Do 18 K, the military version, has earned ill-fame by attacking unarmed lightships and fishing boats.

Fitted with two Junkers 500/560 h.p. " Jumo " 205 water-cooled Diesel engines, mounted in tandem, the maximum speed is 155 m.p.h., cruising speed 136 m.p.h., and range 3,600 miles.

Principal Structural Features

Flying boat, high-wing monoplane, braced. Uniformly tapered wings of large chord, rounded tips, no dihedral. Two in-line engines mounted in tandem above the wing; single fin and rudder, braced tailplane; long slender two-step metal hull, with sponsons.

Special Recognition Points

Wing plan resembles Do 17 and 215 bombers. Tandem engines viewed head-on, resemble single engine, but are very distinctive in side view. Do 18, although about the same length as Consolidated PBY flying boats, has a more slender hull and its wing span is shorter by 26 ft. Note, in plan view, the unusual design of tail unit. Lateral sponsons—or stub wings—built-in to the hull, serve as stabilisers in place of wing floats, and clearly distinguish Dorniers from British flying boats.

DORNIER DO 18
Reconnaissance (or Bomber)
Span 77′ 8″   Length 63′ 2″   Height 17′ 9″

DORNIER 24

Reconnaissance Flying Boat

BUILT by the Dornier-Werke of Friedrichshafen, the Do 24, with slender metal hull fitted with sponsons in place of wing floats, shows a strong family likeness to the Do " Wal " and Do 18 flying boats which in peace time maintained a regular service across the South Atlantic.

The design provides for a power plant consisting of three radial air-cooled engines, each developing about 700/900 h.p. A number of Do 24 flying boats supplied to the Netherlands Government were fitted with Wright Cyclone engines, giving a maximum speed of 211 m.p.h. and a cruising range exceeding 2,000 miles. Those operating with the Luftwaffe are equipped with 880 h.p. BMW, or Bramo " Fafnir " radial engines, developing about 1,000 h.p. Two rotatable gun-turrets can be seen in the lower drawing, one in the nose and another amidships. A third is fitted in the tail. The first Do 24 to be officially reported over England was shot down by A.A. in August, 1940.

Principal Structural Features

Flying boat, high-wing, braced. Centre section of wing is rectangular, outer sections are tapered on leading edge only, with square-cut tips. Three radial engines ; twin fins and rudders ; two-step metal hull with sponsons (stub wings).

Special Recognition Points

Wings of large span, supported centrally by inverted V struts, are braced to lateral sponsons. Marked taper on leading edge only, with square-cut tips ; very slight dihedral on outer section. Three radial engines mounted in line slightly below their centres ; distinctive braced tail unit carried high on slender streamline stern. The angular twin-fins and rudders resemble those of the Do 17 and 215. Glazed turrets in nose, tail and amidships.

DORNIER 24
Reconnaissance
Span 88' 7".   Length 72' 0"   Height 18' 10".

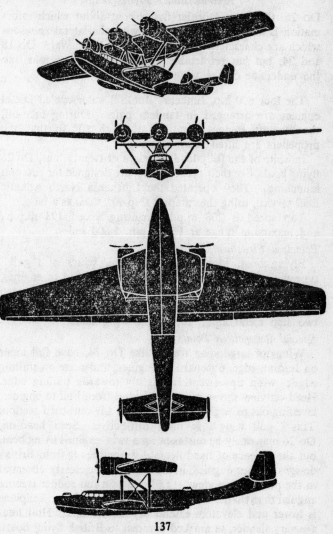

DORNIER 26

Reconnaissance Flying Boat

Do 26, the latest Dornier flying boat about which information is available, is not fitted with the lateral sponsons which are characteristic features of the Do " Wal," Do 18 and 24, but has retractable wing floats. These fold into the underside of the wing during flight.

The four 600 h.p. Junkers " Jumo " water-cooled Diesel engines are arranged in tandem pairs. During take-off, the two aft engines are tilted through 10° so that the propellers are lifted clear of spray.

In spite of the fully-loaded weight of twenty tons, Do 26 flying boats, like their predecessors, are designed for catapult launching. They operated the Lufthansa North Atlantic mail service, using the catapult ship *Friesland* as a base.

Top speed is 208 m.p.h., cruising speed 193 m.p.h., and maximum range at 130 m.p.h. 5,600 miles.

Principal Structural Features

Flying boat, high-wing monoplane, wings of " gull " type with full taper on leading edge, outboard of engines, no taper on trailing edge. Four in-line engines mounted in tandem pairs, single fin and rudder ; braced tailplane ; two step metal hull ; retractable wing-floats.

Special Recognition Points

Wings of large span which, like Do 24, have full taper on leading edge, outboard of engines, and none on trailing edge ; wing tips swept in slightly towards trailing edge. Head-on view shows marked dihedral from hull to engines, levelling out to negligible dihedral on the outboard section. This " gull wing " is most distinctive. Seen head-on, Do 26 may easily be mistaken for a twin-engined flying boat, but the absence of fixed floats distinguishes it from British designs. Four engines, in tandem, can be clearly observed in the plan or side view. Tall single fin and rudder is more angular than that of Do 18 or Consolidated PBY. Tailplane is lower and elevators extend beyond its tips. Hull lines are very slender, in marked contrast to British flying boats.

DORNIER 26
Reconnaissance
Span 98' 0"   Length 80' 5"   Height 22' 5"

SARO "LERWICK"

General Purposes Flying-boat

SUCCESSOR to the "London" biplane flying-boat, built at Cowes by the well-known marine designers, Saunders-Roe Ltd., the "Lerwick" is a monoplane flying-boat not unlike a twin-engined version of the Short "Sunderland." Two Bristol Hercules double-row radial engines of 1,375 h.p. provide the power plant. Performance figures are not released. Armed with three power-operated gun-turrets, it possesses considerable power of attack or defence.

Principal Structural Features

Flying-boat, high-wing monoplane ; outboard of engines the wings taper sharply to semi-pointed tips, with dihedral. Two radial engines, mounted on their centre lines. Tall single fin and rudder ; deep double-deck hull with clearly defined "step" about midway ; fixed wing floats.

Special Recognition Points

Side view : General layout of hull, nose and tail turrets resembles the "Sunderland," but the following points are distinctive : square-cut top of large fin and rudder ; "bite" below rudder where tail turret is mounted ("Sunderland" turret projects aft of tail) ; gun-turret on top of fuselage ; cantilever mounting of wing-floats.

Head-on view : Two engines clearly distinguish the "Lerwick" from the four-engined "Sunderland." Note also the somewhat conical section of the hull, narrow at the top and deep at the base, in contrast to the nearly uniform width (from the same point of view) of the "Sunderland." Nose projects well forward of engines.

SARO LERWICK
General Purposes Flying Boat
Span 80' 10"   Length 63' 7½"   Height 23' 5"

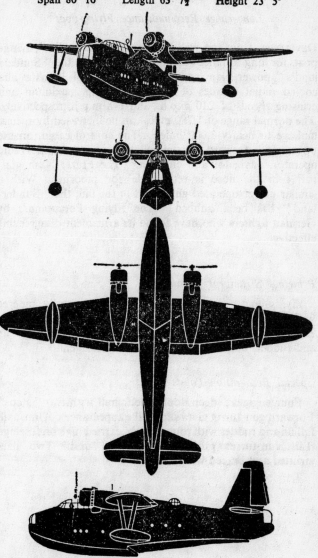

SHORT "SUNDERLAND"

Long-range Reconnaissance Flying-boat

DEVELOPED from the well-known Short " Empire " flying-boats for long distance coastal reconnaissance, the " Sunderland's " power plant consists of four Bristol Pegasus air-cooled radial engines of 850 h.p., giving maximum and cruising speeds of 210 m.p.h., and 178 m.p.h. respectively. The normal range of 1,780 miles can be increased by special tankage to nearly 3,000 miles. The control cabin, on the upper deck forward, accommodates two pilots, the radio operator, navigator and engineer. The Frazer-Nash gun-turret in the nose is retractable for mooring. With a similar power-operated gun-turret in the tail, the " Sunderland " has been dubbed " The Flying Porcupine " by German fighters who have found its armament disagreeably effective.

Principal Structural Features

Flying-boat, high-wing monoplane ; normally tapered wing with slight dihedral and rounded tips. Four radial engines mounted on their centre lines. Single large fin and rudder, tailplane carried high on fuselage.

Special Recognition Points

Four engines ; deep double-deck hull with two " steps." Forward gun-turret gives snout-like appearance. Unusually tall fin and rudder with rounded top, carried high on fuselage. Tail gun-turret projects behind tail unit. Two fixed strutted and braced wing floats.

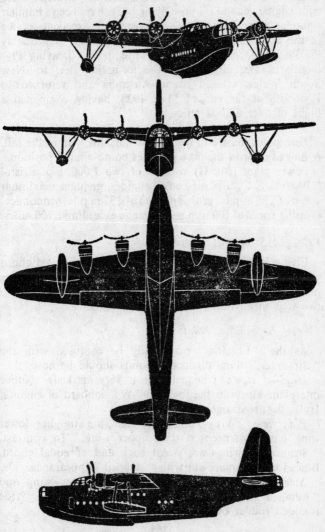

SARO "LONDON"

BUILT by Saunders-Roe, of Cowes, coastal patrols of these twin-engine general purpose flying boats have been a familiar sight for several years. They have given excellent service in the R.A.F., five of them completing what is probably the longest formation flight yet attempted. Leaving Plymouth in December 1937, the formation flew to New South Wales, cruised round Australia and returned to Plymouth at the end of May, 1938, having completed a flight of over 30,000 miles.

Gun positions are in the nose, amidships, and in the tail. A hinged door in the nose provides bomb-aiming position.

Power plant (Mk II) consists of two 1,000 h.p. Bristol "Pegasus X" radial air-cooled engines, giving a maximum speed of 155 m.p.h., cruising speed of 137 m.p.h., economical cruising speed of 109 m.p.h. and range exceeding 1,700 miles.

Principal Structural Features

Flying boat, biplane. Wings of unequal span and chord with rounded tips and slight dihedral. Two radial engines mounted under the upper wing; twin fins and rudders, two-step metal hull; fixed wing-tip floats.

Special Recognition Points

As the "London" may easily be confused with the "Stranraer," these distinctive points should be noted:

Head-on view: Unequal span is very marked. Notice interplane struts in the form of "W" inboard of engines. Hull sides are straight.

Plan view: Wings, of smaller span, are straight; lower wing has shorter chord than upper wing. In contrast, "Stranraer" wings are swept back and of equal chord. Braced tail is square-cut with "stepped" appearance.

Side view: Notice longer chord of upper wing and "humped" appearance of forward control cabin. Wide rounded rudder overhangs the stern.

144

LONDON I (2-Pegasus III)
Reconnaissance
Span 80' 0"   Length 56' 9½"   Height 22' 0"

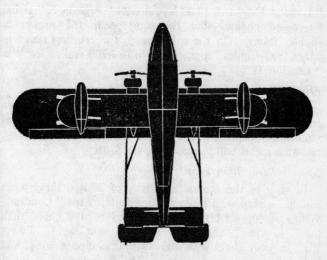

SUPERMARINE "STRANRAER"

Reconnaissance Flying Boat

THIS twin-engine general purpose flying boat is built by the Supermarine Company whose famous high-speed seaplanes distinguished themselves by winning the Schneider Trophy outright for Britain. From the successful Schneider Trophy machine the brilliant "Spitfire" design was developed. The "Stranraer" biplane flying boat does not aspire to "Spitfire" performance, but has several years of R.A.F. patrol and general reconnaissance work to its credit. Like the "London," the "Stranraer" has a machine-gun position and bomb-aiming post in the nose, a machine-gun position amidships and a third gun position in the tail.

The power plant also is similar to that of the Saro "London II"—two 1,000 h.p. Bristol "Pegasus X" radial air-cooled engines—but the top speed, 165 m.p.h. is slightly faster. On the other hand, the cruising range is only 1,000 miles compared with 1,700 miles of the "London II."

Principal Structural Features

Flying boat, biplane. Back-swept wings of unequal span and rounded tips, with slight dihedral. Two radial engines mounted under the upper wing; twin fins and rudders; two-step metal hull; fixed wing-tip floats.

Special Recognition Points

In view of the general similarity of design, these notes should be read with those relating to the Saro "London." Wings of appreciably larger span and smaller chord than the "London" are swept back without taper. Lower wing of only slightly shorter span than upper wing, and both wings have equal chord. The arrangement of interplane struts is simpler. Braced tailplane, untapered, with rounded tips. Tall narrow fins and rudders, which do not overhang the stern. Sides of hull are curved.

STRANRAER (2–Pegasus)
Reconnaissance Flying Boat
Span 85' 0"   Length 54' 6"   Height 23' 3"

SUPERMARINE "WALRUS"

The Supermarine Company, designers of Schneider Trophy winners and of the " Spitfire," fastest fighter in the R.A.F., showed distinct versatility in producing the " Walrus " amphibian flying boat, which is probably the slowest aircraft, excluding initial trainers, operating with the R.A.F.

In service in the Fleet Air Arm since 1935, its chief functions are general reconnaissance and submarine spotting, for which high cruising speeds are unnecessary. The retractable wheeled undercarriage which enables these flying boats to operate over land or sea greatly increases their utility. The " Walrus," designed for catapult launching, is the first amphibian to be catapulted with service load. As the " Seagull V," it has been in service with the Royal Australian Air Force for many years.

Machine-gun cockpits are provided in the bow and aft of the wings. One 775 h.p. Bristol " Pegasus " radial air-cooled engine provides a maximum speed of 135 m.p.h., cruising speed of 95 m.p.h., and range of 600 miles. (Mk. II.)

Principal Structural Features

Flying boat, biplane, amphibian. Wings of equal span without taper, rounded tips, moderate dihedral. Single radial engine, driving pusher air-screw; single fin and rudder; braced tailplane; single-step metal hull; fixed wing tip floats, land undercarriage retracts.

Special Recognition Points

This single-engine flying boat is an unusual and easily recognised type. Note the pusher air-screw driven by uncowled radial engine, which is slung between the single-bay biplane wings. These are swept back to wide rounded tips and are cut away at the centre section of the trailing edge. Large fin and rudder with wide rounded top; braced tailplane of roughly rectangular plan, is mounted near the top of fin. Wheels retract into wells under the wing, leaving undercarriage struts visible.

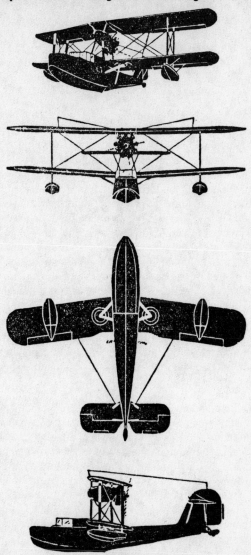

AIRCRAFT SILHOUETTES

SECTION V

BIPLANES - - - - - pp. 152-159
(other than Seaplanes and Flying Boats)

FAIREY " ALBACORE "

ONE of the latest torpedo-spotter-reconnaissance biplanes of the Fleet Air Arm, the " Albacore," operating from aircraft carriers, is an example of modern biplane construction, having folding wings of small span specially designed to save stowage space. Successor to the well-known Fairey " Swordfish," which carried out the brilliant torpedo attack on the Italian fleet at Taranto, it has cleaner lines and is fitted with the more powerful Bristol Taurus sleeve-valve radial engine of 1,065 h.p. Performance figures are not yet officially available. The " Albacore " has taken part in many raids on invasion ports and coastal aerodromes.

Principal Structural Features

Single-bay biplane ; wings of equal span with rounded tips and moderate dihedral. Single radial engine ; single fin and rudder ; fuselage of oval section with fixed undercarriage.

Special Recognition Points

Untapered wings of equal span with rounded tips and trailing edge cut away near fuselage. Tail-plane tapered on leading edge only with rounded tips and large V cut away from the centre section of elevator. The roof of the large glazed cockpit divides the upper wings and projects forward of the leading edge with brow-like effect. Large wide fin and rudder has well-rounded top and distinctive shape ; undercarriage legs are " trousered," but wheels are without " spats."

ALBACORE (Taurus)
Torpedo Spotter Reconnaissance
Span 50′ 0″   Length 40′ 1″   Height 15′ 1″

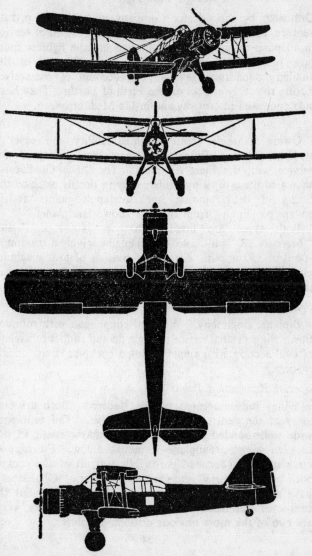

153

"GLADIATOR" and "SEA GLADIATOR"

Single-Seat Fighters

DESIGNED by the Gloster Company in 1934 as a private venture, the "Gladiator" has an excellent record of service in all parts of the world. Although biplane fighters must now be regarded as obsolescent, "Gladiators" of the auxiliary squadrons gave a good account of themselves during the early attacks on the Firth of Forth. They have also done well in Norway and in the Mediterranean.

Owing to their greater manœuvrability and ease of stowage, biplane fighters are particularly adapted for service with the Fleet Air Arm. The "Sea Gladiator" shewn in these drawings differs only in details, such as the fitting of deck landing hook, catapult points and a collapsible dinghy, from the well-known landplane.

Both types are fitted with one 840 h.p. Bristol "Mercury IX" air-cooled radial engine, giving a maximum speed of 250 m.p.h. Armament consists of four machine-guns, two mounted under the lower wings and two fixed in the side of the fuselage.

Principal Structural Features

Biplane, single bay. Wings of equal span with rounded tips. Single radial engine ; single fin and rudder ; fuselage of oval section with single enclosed cockpit ; fixed under-carriage.

Special Recognition Points

Wings fully staggered but not tapered. Both are cut-away at the centre of the trailing edge. Tail unit with wide well-rounded fin and rudder, is characteristic in side or plan views. Tailplane is mounted low. Fuselage of circular section forward is roughly oval aft of the cockpit with "hump" faired into the cockpit cover. "Gladiators" have a family resemblance to the "Gauntlets," but the cantilever (unbraced) undercarriage and single-bay wings are two of the more obvious distinctive points.

SEA GLADIATOR (Mercury)
Single–Seat Fleet Fighter
Span 32' 3"   Length 27' 5"   Height 10' 9½"

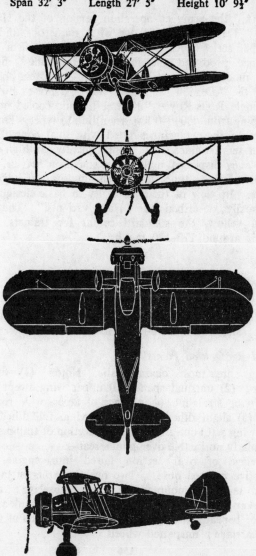

"AUDAX" and "HART VARIANTS"

"AUDAX," the army co-operation version of the Hawker "Hart" Day Bomber, is one of a numerous and distinguished series of R.A.F. biplanes built by the firm which has since produced the famous "Hurricane" fighter. These modifications of the "Hart" two-seat biplane include the "Demon," "Hind" and "Osprey," powered with single Rolls-Royce "Kestrel" liquid-cooled engines developing from 480–640 h.p. according to type. Training versions of these machines fitted with dual control have been in service since 1936. Subsequently, as high-speed monoplanes displaced biplanes in squadron service, large numbers of these types have been employed as advanced trainers. In view of their similarity in basic design they are usually described as "Hart variants." They are painted yellow, the standard colour for trainers. Top speed is around 170–180 m.p.h.

Principal Structural Features

Biplane, single bay. Staggered wings of unequal span, untapered, with rounded tips and dihedral. Single in-line engine ; single fin and rudder ; fixed undercarriage.

Special Recognition Points

Wings are most characteristic. Note: (1) marked stagger ; (2) unequal span ; (3) upper wing swept back, lower wing straight ; (4) absence of taper, wide rounded tips ; (5) slight dihedral of upper wing, full dihedral of lower wing ; (6) cut-away at centre-section of trailing edge, particularly noticeable over pilot's seat.

Fuselage of oval section faired into engine, with distinctive pointed nose. Two open cockpits in tandem. Braced tailplane mounted on top of fuselage ; typical "Hawker" wide fin and rudder with rounded top ; radiator beneath fuselage between forward struts of braced undercarriage ; unspatted wheels.

AUDAX (Kestrel 1B)
Span 37' 3"   Length 29' 6¼"   Height 11' 6"

DE HAVILLAND "TIGER MOTH"

Trainer

PROBABLY more R.A.F. pilots have received their initial training in " Tiger Moths " than in any other type. The first de Havilland " Moth " type D.H. 60, introduced about 1925, rapidly became the most popular light biplane for private owners and the standard training machine of British flying clubs. D.H. 82A, the " Tiger Moth," is a later development, fitted with the more powerful Gipsy " Major " inverted air-cooled in-line engine. This develops 130 h.p. and gives the " Tiger " a top speed of 109 m.p.h., with cruising speed of 93 m.p.h.

Brought into service in the R.A.F. in 1932, the " Tiger Moth " is fitted with dual control and may be equipped with hood and instruments for training in " blind " flying. Extremely manœuvrable, it is fully stressed for aerobatics, and the low stalling speed of 43 m.p.h. provides a high factor of safety. A twin-float version is used as a seaplane trainer. Skis may be substituted for the normal undercarriage.

Principal Structural Features

Biplane, staggered wings swept back, with rounded tips. Single in-line engine ; single fin and rudder ; fuselage of roughly oval section with two seats in tandem. Fixed undercarriage.

Special Recognition Points

Single bay strutted biplane, wings of equal span with marked stagger are swept back without taper to the tips, which are rounded off and swept out to the trailing edge. Slight dihedral. The in-line engine, open cockpits and characteristic de Havilland tail unit, are very distinctive. The latter, in plan, suggests a *moth* with open wings ; in side view, a *moth* with closed wings. Braced tailplane is mounted on top of fuselage. The fixed undercarriage is short, compact and without " spats."

TIGER MOTH (Gipsy III)
Training
Span 29' 4"   Length 23' 11"   Height 8' 9½"

ILLUSTRATED GLOSSARY OF DESCRIPTIVE TERMS

Readers who have more than a passing acquaintance with aircraft design will have no occasion to consult an *A B C* which is intended to assist those members of the wider public who, whilst rapidly becoming air-minded, are not yet completely familiar with the usual descriptive terms. These terms are illustrated by silhouettes of service types of aircraft which possess the described characteristics in a marked degree.

The definitions refer only to the common meaning of the terms when used in connection with aircraft recognition. Readers seeking precise scientific definitions are recommended to consult the standard aeronautical textbooks.

Service spotters are primarily concerned with the general appearance of aircraft in flight, as seen from a considerable distance. In consequence, many of the descriptive terms are frequently used in an approximate sense. Thus " untapered wings with square-cut tips and no dihedral," may accurately convey an observer's general impression of a particular aircraft, although the description may not be in strict agreement with dimensioned drawings.

AEROFOIL.—Term generally used in referring to the wings, ailerons, tailplane, fins, etc., when considered apart from the aeroplane.

AILERONS.—Hinged flaps on the trailing edge of the wings, near to the tips, which provide lateral control. They are so coupled that one is raised as the other is lowered. By this means the pilot executes the movement known as " banking."

DIAGRAM 1

1. Retracted Undercarriage.
2. Engine Cowling.
3. Radial Engine.
4. Slots.
5. Ailerons.
6. Centre Section of Wings.
7. Flaps.
8. Tail Plane.
9. Elevator.

AIR BRAKES.—See Dive Brakes.

AIRSCREW. — General term recommended in preference to " propeller," which means a screw placed at the *stern* pushing the ship along. The " pusher " type of airscrew is less common than the " tractor " type. The latter, placed in front, " pulls " an aeroplane through the air.

AIRSCREW DISC OR RADIUS.—The area, or radius, of the circle swept by the airscrew blades. When guns fire through the airscrew disc their speed of operation must be synchronised with the rotating airscrew by the use of interrupter gear. This reduces the rate of fire.

AIRSCREW SPINNER.—A streamline cap, usually in light alloy, which is fitted over the flat central " boss " of an airscrew in order to reduce head resistance.

AMPHIBIAN.—A type of aircraft which, being provided with a hull or floats in addition to a wheeled undercarriage, can operate from land or water.

ANHEDRAL.—Or " negative dihedral," is the angle between each wing and the horizontal when the wings are inclined *downwards* towards the tips. (See Dihedral.)

ASPECT RATIO.—The ratio of span to chord, represented by $\dfrac{\text{span}}{\text{chord}}$.

Example.—40-feet span divided by 5-feet chord equals aspect ratio of 8. In the case of tapered or elliptical wing forms where *chord* varies, the numerical value is obtained by dividing the square of *span* by the *wing area*. $\left(\dfrac{\text{Span}^2}{\text{Wing area}}\right)$.

DIAGRAM 2

B. Special Bomb Containers on the Wellesley.

Sailplane wings have very high aspect ratio. The Wellington is an example of a heavy bomber with high aspect ratio wings, the value being nearly 10. The Wellesley ratio of 8·8 is also high. The Flamingo, around 7·5, is moderate, whilst the Hurricane, about 6·2, and the Whitley, 5·8, are examples of rather low aspect ratio.

BACKSWEPT.—See Sweepback.

BALANCE, MASS OR STATIC.—The arrangement of hinged control surfaces, such as rudders and elevators, in such a way that the moment of the part forward of the hinge balances that of the after part.

BALANCE, AERODYNAMIC. — The arrangement of hinged control surfaces so that the pressure of the airflow on the smaller area forward of the hinge tends to balance the pressure on the main control surface behind the hinge.

BAY.—Biplane wings are supported by interplane struts which subdivide the span into sections termed "bays."

"BITE."—Self-explanatory term used to indicate a curved indentation. (See Cut-away.)

BRACED.—Usually refers to bracing wires or rods, but is also used in a wider sense to describe surfaces supported by struts or other external members, e.g. "braced tailplane," as opposed to the more modern "cantilever" construction. (See Cantilever.)

CAMBER.—The curvature of the upper or lower surface of a wing or of any aerofoil.

CANTILEVER.—A method of construction applied chiefly to wings, fins, tailplanes and undercarriage, in which no external struts, braces or supports are employed. Cantilever construction gives clean lines with low head resistance. As it is normally employed for the wings, fins and tail-plane of modern aircraft, the term is rarely used in the descriptive notes. Cantilever construction may be assumed in all cases where these components are not specifically described as "strutted" or "braced."

DIAGRAM 3
1. Radial Engine.
2. Wings of equal span with Rounded Tips.
3. "Unspatted" Wheels.
4. Cantilever Undercarriage.
5. "Single Bay" Biplane.

CEILING (ABSOLUTE).—Height beyond which the aircraft cannot climb, and at which only one speed of flight is possible.

CEILING (SERVICE).—Height beyond which the rate of climb falls below 100 feet per minute.

CHORD.—Width of wing or aerofoil from leading to trailing edge measured in a straight line, disregarding camber.

CONSERVATORY. — Colloquial description of the large glazed roof enclosing the cabin of certain 'planes, e.g. Anson, Battle, etc. Also termed " greenhouse."

COWLING.—Sheet metal cover of streamline form which more or less encloses the engine. On radial engines the cowling is usually combined with an exhaust collector ring and air-cooling ducts.

CUT-AWAY.—Denotes that the regular outline of a wing or elevator is cut away, for example, to enlarge the pilot's field of view or to give rudder clearance.

DIAGRAM 4

1. Anhedral Angle.
2. Dihedral Angle.
3. Dive Brakes.
4. Inverted Gull-Wings.

DIHEDRAL.—Or " positive dihedral," is the angle between each wing and the horizontal when the wings are inclined *upwards* towards the tips. (See Anhedral.)

DIVE BRAKES.—Flaps, special fairings or other movable surfaces which in normal flight lie parallel to the airflow. During a dive these " air brakes " can be turned through 90° to increase head resistance, thereby reducing the diving speed. (See Flaps.)

164

ELEVATOR.—The hinged portion of the tailplane by means of which the pilot climbs, dives or keeps his craft in level flight, i.e. maintains longitudinal control.

FAIRING.—Light covering of streamline form fitted to reduce resistance to airflow. Undercarriage legs so enclosed are colloquially described as " trousered." Wheels partially enclosed in fairings are " spatted." (See Fillet.)

FILLET.—An extension of the wing, fin or other surface at the point of attachment to the fuselage. Usually curved and of streamline form, it is another type of fairing designed to improve airflow. (See Fairing.)

FIN.—The fixed vertical part of the tail unit, to which the rudder is usually hinged. Like the fin of a fish or the keel of a boat, it increases directional and lateral stability.

FLAPS.—Movable surfaces at the trailing edge, so arranged that their position and angle in relation to the trailing edge may be controlled by the pilot. They serve as air brakes, enabling the pilot to steepen the landing glide without gaining excessive speed, or as dive brakes. As variable camber devices they improve " lift " at low speeds, providing increased safety and control during take-off and landing. (See Dive Brakes.)

FLOAT.—A buoyant watertight support resembling an elongated boat which is fitted to the undercarriage of seaplanes. Fitted to the underside of the wings of flying-boats, floats serve as stabilisers, preventing damage to the wings in a heavy sea.

DIAGRAM 5

1. In-line Engine.
2. Coupé-type Enclosed Cockpit.
3. Fin.
4. Rudder.
5. Tail-wheel.
6. Radiator.
7. Tractor Airscrew.
8. Spinner.

FLOAT SEAPLANE.—An aeroplane, designed for operating from water, in which floats replace wheels.

FLYING-BOAT.—An aeroplane, designed for long overseas flights, in which a seaworthy hull replaces the fuselage and float undercarriage of a seaplane.

DIAGRAM 6

1. Wings swept back.
2. Pusher Airscrew.
3. Fixed Wing Tip Floats.
4. Wheels retracted into Wells underneath Wings.
5. Hull.

FLYING WING.—See Fuselage.

FUSELAGE.—The body of an aeroplane in which the pilot, crew and load are accommodated and to which other main structural parts are attached. In the " flying-wing " type, the fuselage is merged into the centre section of a single large wing of special design.

GAP.—The distance between the upper and lower planes of a biplane.

GEODETIC CONSTRUCTION.—The Vickers-Wallis system in which a curved lattice-work of light alloy girders replaces heavy spars and ribs in the construction of wings, fuselage, etc. The name is derived from " geodetic " line, i.e. the shortest line joining two points lying along the surface of a sphere.

GULL-WINGS.—Wings which have marked dihedral angle near to the fuselage, changing abruptly to little or no dihedral towards the tips and resembling the outspread wings of a gull. Inverted gull-wings have marked anhedral (negative dihedral) near the fuselage, with more or less full dihedral throughout the remainder of their span.

166

IN-LINE ENGINES. — Consisting of one or more blocks of cylinders arranged in line as in motor-car engines. The Rolls-Royce " Merlin " is an in-line V-type liquid-cooled engine, the two blocks of six cylinders in line being arranged in V form. The Napier " Dagger " air-cooled engine has four in-line blocks, each of six cylinders, arranged approximately in H form.

INVERTED GULL-WINGS. — See Gull-Wings.

LEADING EDGE. — The forward edge of wings, tailplane, fins, etc.

MONOCOQUE CONSTRUCTION. — Term applied to fuselage built in a single shell around formers which are spaced along its length.

NACELLES. — Streamline housings outside the fuselage which usually enclose the engines of a multi-engined aircraft.

NEGATIVE DIHEDRAL. — See Anhedral and Dihedral.

PROPELLER. — See Airscrew.

PUSHER AIRSCREW. — See Airscrew.

RADIAL ENGINE. — That type of engine in which the cylinders are arranged radially around a central crankshaft. In contrast to the older type of rotary engine, the cylinder block is stationary, whilst the crank revolves. Usually air-cooled, radial engines are partially enclosed in a streamline cowling of circular section. The most numerous types consist of a single row of seven or nine cylinders arranged star-wise. Later types, termed " twin-row " or " double-row " radials, consist of fourteen or eighteen cylinders arranged radially in two rows.

DIAGRAM 7

1. Leading Edge (Wing).
2. Glazed Bomb-aiming Nose.
3. Radiator and Nacelle.
4. " Bite " out of Trailing Edge.
5. Elliptical Tail Plane.
6. Elevator.
7. Trailing Edge.
8. Leading Edge (Tail Plane).
9. Under Gun Position.
10. Trailing Edge (Wing).

RETRACTABLE (*Float, Gun-Turret, Undercarriage*)—Capable of being drawn up or folded under the aircraft during flight in order to reduce head resistance.

DIAGRAM 8
1. Fairing.
2. Rudder.
3. Braced Tail Plane.
4. Deck Landing Hook.
5. Cantilever Undercarriage.
6. Airscrew Disc.
7. Staggered Wings (Upper Wing Forward of Lower Wing).

RUDDER. — Movable control surface hinged at the fin, which in normal flying attitude is vertical and, like the rudder of a boat, provides directional control. When an aeroplane is banked, the rudder, no longer vertical, exchanges functions with the elevator in proportion as the angle of bank is increased.

SEMI-RETRACTABLE UNDER-CARRIAGE.—Undercarriage, of which the wheels are only partly retracted, enabling a safe landing to be made should the extending mechanism fail to operate.

DIAGRAM 9
1. " Conservatory."
2. Gun Turret.
3. Fin.
4. Rudder.
5. Tail Plane.
6. Semi-retracted Wheels.
7. Fluted Cowling.
8. Nose of Fuselage.

SESQUIPLANE.—A biplane in which one of the main planes is very much smaller than the other. Literally " one-and-a-half " planes.

SLAB-SIDED. — Self-explanatory term applied to the type of fuselage which, although not fully rectangular in section, has flat sides.

SLOTS.—Small slats of streamline section, fitted near to the leading edge of the wings. In normal flight they remain closed, but open automatically at low speeds forming a narrow slot which induces a better flow of air over the wing surface. The " lift " of the wing is thereby increased, and the stalling speed of the aircraft proportionately reduced. Fixed slots consist of a series of small slots, permanently open, arranged near the leading edge of the wing.

DIAGRAM 10
1. Radial Engine with Fluted Cowling.
2. Parasol Wing with Sweep Back.
3. Trailing Edge " cut away."
4. Braced Tail Plane.
5. Fixed Undercarriage, " Spatted " Wheels.
6. Spinner.

SPAN.—The distance between the extreme tips of the longest main plane.

" SPATTED " UNDERCARRIAGE.—See Fairings.

SPONSON.—See Stub Wings.

STAGGER.—When the upper wings of a biplane are forward of the lower wings they are said to be staggered. This arrangement, also termed forward or positive stagger, is quite common. The opposite arrangement, in which the upper wings are behind, termed backward or negative stagger, is unusual.

DIAGRAM 11

1. Three Radial Engines
2. Tapered Leading Edge.
3. Square-cut Wing Tips.
4. Sponsons or Stub Wings.
5. Flying-boat Hull.

STALLING SPEED.—The speed at which the flying controls become ineffective and the lift derived from airflow is insufficient to sustain flight.

STREAMLINE.—So shaped as to produce the least resistance to the airflow.

SWEEPBACK. — Term describing the angular setting of wings, viewed in plan. Wings which have sweepback are inclined towards the tail. (Should not be confused with taper.)

STUB WINGS.—Also termed " sponsons." Very short wings, little more than stubby wing-roots, built on to the hull of flying-boats near the water-line. They are a distinctive feature of Dornier and of certain American flying-boats. Stub wings have a stabilising effect in a heavy sea, and in this respect replace wing floats.

TAIL.—The tailplane and elevators of an aircraft. Also used in a wider sense, meaning the extremity of the fuselage and or the tail unit.

TAILPLANE.—The fixed part of the horizontal control surfaces at the after end of the fuselage.

TAIL UNIT.—The complete assembly of the tailplane(s), elevator(s), fin(s), and rudder(s).

TANDEM.—(In tandem.) Arranged in line one behind the other.

TRACTOR AIRSCREW. — See Airscrew.

TRAILING EDGE.—The rearward edge of the wings, tailplane, fins, etc.

" TROUSERED " UNDERCARRIAGE —See Fairings.

TWIN TAIL.—Compound tail unit having two fins and two rudders.

INDEX

With abbreviated description of principal structural features.

ABBREVIATIONS

Principal Groups :   LW :   Low-wing monoplane.

MW : Mid-wing monoplane, including L.mw. : Low mid-wing.

HW : High-wing monoplane, including Sh.w. : Shoulder wing.

Fl. bt. : Flying-boat.   S.pl. : Seaplane.

Amph. : Amphibian.   Ff. : Floats fixed.   Fr. : Floats retract.   Sp : Sponsons or stub wings.

Bi : Biplane.

Number of Engines :   E1, E2, E3, E4, etc.

Tail Unit :   T1 : Simple, i.e. single fin and rudder.

T2 : compound, i.e. two or more fins and/or rudders.

2 bms : Twin tail booms.

T2/3 : Compound tail with three fins and/or rudders.

Type of Engine :   Re : Radial engine.   Le : In-line engine.

Type of Under-carriage :   Uf : Undercarriage fixed.   Uf (Flt) : Float plane.

Uf (3 Flt) : Float plane central float.

Uf/2 × 2 : 2 side-by-side pairs wheels.

Uf/2 tan prs : 2 prs tandem wheels.

Ur : Undercarriage retracts.   Ur/3 : Tricycle undercarriage, i.e. with single front wheel.

Country of Origin :   A. : Australia.   B. : Belgium.   C. : Canada. F. : France.   G. : Germany.   G.B. : Great Britain.   H. : Holland.   I. : Italy.   U.S.A. : United States of America.

Name	Struc-tural Group.	Country of Origin.	Structural Features.	Page.
Albacore - -	V	G.B.	Bi, E1, Tl, Re, Uf -	152–53
Anson - - -	I	G.B.	Lw, E2, Tl, Re, Ur	60–1
Audax - - -	V	G.B.	Bi, El, Tl, Le, Uf -	156–57
Battle - - -	I	G.B.	LW, El, Tl, Le, Ur	52–3
Beaufort - -	II	G.B.	Mw, E2, Tl, Re, Ur	82–3
Blenheim I - -	II	G.B.	MW, E2, Tl, Re, Ur	84–5
Blenheim IV -	II	G.B.	MW, E2, Tl, Re, Ur	88–9
Blohm & Voss Ha 138	IV	G.	Fl bt, HW, E3, T2 (2 bms), Le, Ff	130–31
Blohm & Voss Ha 139	IV	G.	S.pl, LW, E4, T2, Le, Uf (flt)	126–27
Blohm & Voss Ha 140	IV	G.	S.pl, MW, E2, T2, Re, Uf (flt)	128–29
Blohm & Voss Ha 142	I	G.	LW, E4, T2, Re, Ur	74–5
Bolingbroke - -	II	C.	MW, E2, Tl, Re, Ur	88–9
Bombay - -	III	G.B.	HW, E2, T2, Re, Uf	118–19
Boston - - -	III	U.S.A.	HW (Sh), E2, T1, Re, Ur/3	108–9
Brewster 339 - Brewster F2A–2 - Buffalo - - - Consolidated P.B.Y.5	II	U.S.A.	MW, E1, T1, Re, Ur	78–9
Consolidated 28/5 - (R.A.F. Catalina)	IV	U.S.A.	Fl bt, HW, E2, T1, Re, Fr	132–33
Consolidated 28/5A	IV	U.S.A.	Fl. bt, Amph, HW, E2, T1, Re, Ur, Fr	132–33
Defiant - -	I	G.B.	LW, E1, T1, Le, Ur	44–5
Demon - -	V	G.B.	Bi, E1, Tl, Le, Uf -	156–7
Dornier X - -	IV	G.	Fl Bt, HW, E12 (tan), T1, L & Re, Sp	134
Dornier Wal - -	IV	G.	Fl bt, HW, E2 (tan), T1, Le, Sp	134
Dornier 17 - -	III	G.	HW (Sh), E2, T2, L & Re, Ur	112–15
Dornier 18 - -	IV	G.	Fl bt, HW, E2 (tan), T1, Le, Sp	134–35
Dornier 24 - -	IV	G.	Fl bt, HW, E3, T2, Re, Sp	136–37
Dornier 26 - -	IV	G.	Fl bt, HW, E4 (tan), T1, Le, Fr	138–39
Dornier 215 - -	III	G.	HW (Sh), E2, T2, L & Re, Ur	116–17
Douglas A.20 -	III	U.S.A.	HW (Sh), E2, T1, Re, Ur/3	108–9
Douglas D.B.7 -	III	U.S.A.	HW (Sh), E2, T1, Re, Ur/3	108–9

Name	Struc-tural Group	Country of Origin	Structural Features	Page
Flamingo - -	III	G.B.	HW, E2, T2, Re, Ur	110–11
Gladiator - -	V.	G.B.	Bi, E1, T1, Re, Uf -	154–55
Hampden - -	II	G.B.	MW, E2, T2, Re, Ur	92–5
Harrow - -	III	G.B.	HW, E2, T2, Re, Uf	120–21
Hart - -	V	G.B.	Bi, E1, T1, Le, Uf -	156–57
Harvard - -	I	U.S.A.	LW, E1, T1, Re, Ur	56–7
Heinkel III -	I	G.	LW, E2, T1, Le, Ur	62–3
Heinkel 112 -	I	G.	LW, E1, T1, Le, Ur	38–9
Heinkel 113 -	I	G.	LW, E1, T1, Le, Ur	38–9
Heinkel 115 -	IV	G.	S.pl, MW, E2, T1, Re, Ff	124–5
Henschel 126 -	III	G.	HW, E1, T1, Re, Uf	106–7
Hereford -	II	G.B.	MW, E2, T2, Le, Ur	92–5
Hertfordshire -	III	G.B.	HW, E2, T2, Re, Ur	110–11
Hind - -	V	G.B.	Bi, E1, T1, Le, Uf -	156–7
Hudson - -	II	U.S.A.	MW (Lmw), E2, T2, Re, Ur	96–7
Hurricane - -	I	G.B.	LW, E1, T1, Le, Ur	40–1
Junkers 52/3m -	I	G.	LW, E3, T1, Re, Uf	66–7
Junkers 86 -	I	G.	LW, E2, T2, Re, Ur	70–1
Junkers 86K -	I	G.	LW, E2, T2, L & Re, Ur	70–1
Junkers 87 -	I	G.	LW, E1, T1, Le, Uf	46–47
Junkers 88 -	II	G.	MW (Lmw), E2, T1, Le (radial cowl), Ur	86–7
Junkers 89 -	I	G.	LW, E4, T2, Le, Ur	72–3
Junkers 90 -	I	G.	LW, E4, T2, Re, Ur	72–3
Lerwick - -	IV	G.B.	Fl. bt. HW, E2, T1, Re, Ff	140–41
Lockheed 14 -	II	U.S.A.	MW (Lmw), E2, T2, Re, Ur	96–7
London - -	IV	G.B.	Fl. bt. Bi, E2, T2, Re, Ff	144–45
Lysander - -	III	G.B.	HW, E1, T1, Re, Uf	104–5
Magister - -	I	G.B.	LW, E1, T1, Le, Uf	58–9
Master - -	I	G.B.	LW, E1, T1, Le, Ur	54–5
Messerschmitt 109	I	G.	LW, E1, T1, Le, Ur	42–3
Messerschmitt 110	I	G.	LW, E2, T2, Le, Ur	68–9
Messerschmitt Jaguar	I	G.	LW, E2, T2, Le, Ur	68–9
Moth - -	V	G.B.	Bi, E1, T1, Le, Uf -	158–59
North American B.C.1 - -	I	U.S.A.	LW, E1, TI, Re, Ur	56–7
North American NA.16-3	I	U.S.A.	LW, E1, T1, Re, Ur	56–7
Osprey - - -	V	G.B.	Bi, E1, T1, Le, Uf -	156–7

Name	Structural Group	Country of Origin	Structural Features	Page
Oxford - - -	I	G.B.	LW, E2, T1, Re, Ur	64–5
Roc - - -	I	G.B.	LW, E1, T1, Re, Ur	50–1
Sea Gladiator -	V	G.B.	Bi, E1, T1, Re, Uf -	154–55
Seagull V - -	IV	G.B.	Fl. bt. Amph, Bi, E1, T1, Re, Ur, Ff	148–49
Skua - - -	I	G.B.	LW, E1, T1, Re, Ur	48–9
Spitfire - -	I	G.B.	LW, E1, T1, Le, Ur	36–37
Stranraer - -	IV	G.B.	Fl. bt. Bi, E2, T2, Re, Ff	146–47
Sunderland - -	IV	G.B.	Fl. bt. E4, T1, Re, Ff	142–43
Tiger Moth - -	V	G.B.	Bi, E1, T1, Le, Uf -	158–59
Walrus - - -	IV	G.B.	Fl. bt. Amph, Bi, E1, T1, Re, Ur, Ff	148–49
Wellesley - -	II	G.B.	MW (Lmw), E1, T1, Re, Ur	80–1
Wellington - -	II	G.B.	MW, E2, T1, L. & Re, Ur	90–1
Whitley Mk I–III -	II	G.B.	MW, E2, T2, Re, Ur	98–101
Whitley Mk IV–V -	II	G.B.	MW, E2, T2, Le, Ur	98–101
Wirraway - -	I	A.	LW, E1, T1, Re, Ur	56–7